JUST IN TIME!

BAPTISM SERVICES, SERMONS, AND PRAYERS

Kenneth H. Carter Jr.

D1531107

Abingdon Press
Nashville

JUST IN TIME!
BAPTISM SERVICES, SERMONS, AND PRAYERS

This book is printed on acid-free paper.

Library of Congress Cataloging-in-Publication Data

Carter, Kenneth H.
    Baptism services, sermons, and prayers / Kenneth H. Carter, Jr.
       p. cm.—(Just in time!)
    ISBN 0-687-33383-0 (binding: pbk., adhesive perfect : alk. paper)
    1. Baptism—Baptists. 2. Baptists—Liturgy—Texts. 3. Worship
programs. I. Title. II. Series: Just in time! (Nashville, Tenn.)
BX6339.B37C37   2006
265'.1—dc22

                                                                            2006003468

06 07 08 09 10 11 12 13 14 15—10 9 8 7 6 5 4 3 2 1

MANUFACTURED IN THE UNITED STATES OF AMERICA

CONTENTS

116601

Contents

INTRODUCTION

Ernest Campbell, former minister of the Riverside Church in
New York City, once called pastors to consider "energizing
the usual" rather than "scheduling the unusual." When we
give care, attention, and creativity to the ritual of Christian baptism, we are "energizing the usual." In the history of Christianity,
certain practices have been the occasion upon which the faithful
have encountered God. These practices are channels of grace,
movements of the Spirit. One of these practices is Christian baptism.

This book is a resource for pastors and worship leaders who
take Christian baptism seriously, who trust in God's faithfulness
to the traditional means of grace, and yet who also recognize our
own role in shaping these practices. The three chapters within
include worship resources for a variety of pastoral and congregational settings, a number of teaching sermons, and a series of
prayers of thanksgiving over the waters of baptism. The chapters
correspond to the roles of pastor, preacher, and liturgist. They are
shaped (but not limited by) the Christian calendar, community,
and canon. The resources invite your own response and transla-
tion. They call forth your own vision and creativity.

Our world is divided in many ways, and the church often mir-
rors these divisions. The ritual (sacrament) of baptism is the one
experience shared by all Christians. Our humanity is marred by
sin and brokenness, and people of faith yearn for a new existence.
The ritual (sacrament) of baptism is the one experience that
promises cleansing of the heart and wholeness of the Spirit.

I write in gratitude for my own baptism, almost thirty years ago
now, by Dr. Jerry Johnson at Mount Zion Baptist Church in

Columbus, Georgia; in remembrance of the baptism of our children: Elizabeth, at the Memorial Chapel, Lake Junaluska, North Carolina, by Bishop L. Bevel Jones, III and Abby, at Christ Church (United Methodist) in Greensboro, North Carolina, by Rev. Skip Parvin; and in appreciation for the community of the baptized who worship at Providence United Methodist Church, Charlotte, North Carolina.

May the spoken word voiced in worship echo the word of God, claiming us as sons and daughters. May the gathered people of God claim the grace and live into the promises of their baptisms. May the life-giving waters, clearly visible in our presence, be a reminder of the promise of the New Testament: the God who began a good work in you will be faithful to complete it (Philippians 1:6).

PART ONE

BAPTISM AND CONGREGATIONAL LIFE

Baptism is an "outward and visible sign of an inward and spiritual grace." It is an external action that points to something within—hopefully, an experience of God. At times, the church offers services of baptism or baptismal renewal. At other times, individuals seek out a pastor for the baptism of their child. And at other times, individuals who are drawing nearer to God inquire about the possibility of their own baptisms.

Baptism is about connecting the life-giving waters of God (John 4:14) with the presence of the gathered community and the faithful person. As church leaders recognize, these three elements—water, gathered community, and personal faith—are also related to particular life situations and to the flow of the Christian and civic calendars. For this reason, the thoughtful pastor and worship leader will give attention to these variables, while upholding his or her ordination vows to stand within the integrity of a particular tradition.

Through Christian baptism we are made a part of God's covenant people. By the gift of water we are incorporated into the body of Christ. Baptism is a gift to the whole church, and not to a particular denomination. I have written this book for pastors and worship leaders across a broad spectrum of denominations. Some have the practice of infant baptism; others do not. The

1

reader is invited to translate these liturgies, prayers, and teaching sermons into his or her own setting.

In this chapter, I have offered a number of different resources. Underneath them all is a conviction that ritual orders our life together. We need this ritual of baptism so that we can stay close to the gift of God's grace. And yet I am also convinced that rituals can be adapted to fit the needs of individuals and congregations. And so the act of baptism must be related to life stages, parish situations, and congregational needs.

LIFE STAGES

The Baptism of Infants

In interpreting the baptism of an infant, Romans 5:8 is particularly helpful: "God proves his love for us in that while we still were sinners Christ died for us." The baptism of an infant is a sign of God's grace that goes before our human response.

Since infants will be unaware of their own baptisms, it is important that they be given a document that will interpret the experience for them at a later date. Many pastors write a letter similar to the following, which can be read or opened upon their confirmation of profession of faith:

Dear (<u>Name</u>):

Several years ago you were baptized at (<u>Church Name</u>) Church in (<u>City, State</u>). You were too young to remember the service, or the events that surrounded it. This was, however, a very important day in your life, and in the lives of your parents, and the congregation that gathered that day.

On the day of your baptism, your parents stood before the church, held you in their loving arms, and reaffirmed their faith in Jesus Christ. They also promised to teach you the Christian faith through example, study of Scripture, and participation in the life of the church. The congregation then promised to support your parents in their faith, and to help to guide you toward discipleship as a follower of Jesus.

Baptism is a very simple act. The water that was placed on your head symbolized God's cleansing of sin and gift of new life, promised to those who are blessed with this sacrament (ritual).

The baptism of a child is in part about the grace of God that goes before our human response. God has been at work in your life from the very beginning! But baptism is also a sign that points toward the future, and your own acceptance of Christ through profession of faith.

As you now confess your own personal faith in Jesus Christ, I hope you will look back upon your baptism as a gift that has made your response possible. Give thanks for the faith of your parents and the church that surrounded them. Continue to nourish your relationship with Christ and the church. May the grace of God continue to sustain you in all the days of your life.

The peace of the Lord,
(Name), pastor

The Baptism of Youth

Many young people enter into the fellowship of local churches without any prior congregational participation. If they have not been baptized, this is a gift that can be crucial in the faith development of a young person. Young people are especially open to the movements of God in their lives and in need of the traditional practices of Christian faith, including baptism.

Prior to Baptism

The mentor (or pastor) meets with the young person to explain the meaning of baptism. This conversation can include:

- Discussion of several Scripture passages (See part 2 of this book for ideas).
- Attention to the meaning of the baptism of Jesus.
- A time for response to questions such as:
  ○ Will baptism keep me from going to hell (or insure that I go to heaven)? *These matters are not the stated purpose of baptism in Scripture.*
  ○ Does it matter if I am immersed or sprinkled? *In Scripture, baptism seems to happen with both methods.*

- ○ What does baptism mean? *Respond with comments about new life, cleansing, forgiveness, and God's use of water in the history of salvation.*
- Noting that baptism is incorporation into the church and not merely a personal or private experience.
- Discussion of the relation of baptism to other practices (such as Holy Communion, service, etc.).
- Answers to any practical questions the young person might have (which family members to invite, what will happen in the service, etc.).

If this baptism occurs in the midst of a confirmation service, the prior conversation will be helpful. Pray with the young person that they will be receptive to God's spirit and grace.

Following the Baptism

- Ask the baptized young person to write a page about what the experience meant to them. Ask him or her to be specific!
- Ask the young person how his or her relationship to Christ and the church has been since the ritual. This will open the door to a conversation about spiritual highs and lows.
- Ask the young person to make a commitment to at least one traditional Christian practice, such as the study of Scripture, or prayer, or service, or singing in a choir.
- Pray for the young person, that he or she will be faithful to his or her promises to God and to the church.
- Give the young person a small gift—a Bible, a devotional book, a CD of Christian music, or something that is more personal—as a sign of your care for them and for their spiritual journey.

This mentoring relationship, and the young person's participation in the church, will be essential as she or he grows in the faith. For an excellent reflection on the church's ministry with youth, see *The Godbearing Life: The Art of Soul Tending for Youth*

Ministry by Kenda Creasy Dean and Ron Foster (Upper Room Books, 1998).

A Prayer for a Young Person, upon His or Her Baptism

God of grace,
You love us even when we feel unloved.
You accept us even when we are imperfect.
You have a plan and a purpose for us.
Gather (*Name*) into the arms of your embrace.
Help him/her always to know that you walk beside hm/her.
May the waters of baptism
Be a sign of your love for him/her,
And the mark of your salvation
Throughout all the days of his/her life.
In Jesus' name; Amen.

The Baptism of Adults

If an adult has not been baptized, the ritual is connected to their profession of faith. Often, adults have experiences that lead them to the desire for forgiveness, reconciliation, and a new beginning. Water is wonderfully symbolic of these desires and is a sign of God's gift of grace. A conversation prior to the baptism and following will be helpful.

Prior to Baptism

The mentor (or pastor) meets with the adult to explain the meaning of baptism. This conversation can include:
- Discussion of several Scripture passages (including those in the section of sermons in this book).
- Attention to the meaning of the baptism of Jesus.
- A time for listening to the life story of the adult. Often, significant experiences may provide clues about movements of the spirit in his or her life. The sharing of these experiences by the candidate can be a form of testimony.

- Reading Romans 6:1-11 together.
- Noting that baptism is incorporation into the church and not merely a personal or private experience. It will be important that the candidate makes a covenant to participate in worship and, ideally, in a small group.
- Asking if the candidate has any questions about the service itself.
- Prayer with the adult, giving thanks for God's grace and for the candidate's openness to the movement of the Spirit.

Following the Baptism

- Ask the baptized adult to write a page about what the experience meant. Ask him or her to be specific!
- Ask the adult how her or his relationship to Christ and the church has been since the ritual. This will open the door to a conversation about spiritual highs and lows.
- Ask the adult to make a commitment to at least one traditional Christian practice, such as the study of Scripture, or prayer, or service, or singing in a choir, for a distinct period or time. Speak of this as a way of "living the baptismal vows or promises."
- Pray for the adult, that he or she will be faithful to his or her promises to God and to the church.

A Prayer for an Adult, upon Her or His Baptism

God of grace and mercy,
You make all things new.
I thank you for my brother/sister (*Name*).
I thank you for the cleansing waters of baptism.
I thank you that forgiveness is possible.
Mostly I thank you for Jesus Christ,
And for the gift of baptism in his name. Amen.

THE COMMUNITY'S RESPONSE

Standing with the Baptized

Baptism is a corporate experience, and is best situated in the worship of the gathered community. How does your congregation participate in baptism? Some churches sing "Blest Be the Tie That Binds," or "Jesus Loves Me," as a response. Others applaud as a sign of encouragement to the parents. Others join hands as the pastor prays for the baptized or for the baptized and his or her parents. Others offer gifts: a prayer shawl, or a Bible with names of members written inside, or a rainbow bookmark.

Welcoming the Child into the Community: Hospitality

When a child enters into a family, everything is rearranged! When a child is baptized, the congregation makes room for this new person. The importance of hospitality is central to the act of baptism. Pastors and worship leaders often speak of the newly baptized and our calling to care for them in nurseries, to teach them in Sunday school classes, to shepherd them in youth ministries. How welcoming are we to children and young people?

Representing the Body: The Lay Leader

It is wonderfully symbolic when a lay leader participates in the ritual of baptism. While the clergy performs the baptism and recites the words, a lay leader can represent the congregation in offering hospitality and extending a gentle challenge to the parents to keep their own promises. A representative leader reminds everyone present that baptism is incorporation into the body of Christ.

No Solitary Christians:
The Response of the Congregation

Many traditions have particular spoken responses for the gathered congregation within the service of baptism. For example, the following is a part of United Methodist services of baptism:

> Now it is our joy to welcome our new *sisters* and *brothers* in Christ.
> **Through baptism**
> **you are incorporated by the Holy Spirit into God's new creation**
> **and made to share in Christ's royal priesthood.**
> **We are all one in Christ Jesus.**
> **With joy and thanksgiving we welcome you as *members* of the family of Christ.**
> (*The United Methodist Hymnal*, from *Baptismal Covenants I, II*
> © 1976, 1980, 1985, 1989 United Methodist Publishing House.
> Used by permission)

This response is a reminder that there are no solitary Christians and that baptism is a communal act, one shared by all disciples of Jesus Christ.

Reaffirmation of Vows:
Reminders of Our Promises

Throughout this book the reader will reflect on both baptism and baptismal renewal. As human beings, we are often prone to forget important truths (see Deuteronomy 6:12). Visible reminders are helpful, and most congregations welcome occasional services that offer the ritual of baptismal renewal. These services will be most effective if the preacher and the liturgists interpret them.

Singing the Faith

The following hymns and choruses are appropriate to the setting of baptism. You may consult the hymnal in your own tradition for additional possibilities:

- "The Church's One Foundation"
- "Wash O God, Our Sons and Daughters"
- "Come Let Us Use the Grace Divine"
- "This Is the Spirit's Entry Now"
- "Child of Blessing, Child of Promise"
- "There Is a Fountain"
- "God Claims You"
- "Wade in the Water"
- "I Was There to Hear Your Borning Cry"
- "Spirit of the Living God"
- "When Jesus Came to Jordan"
- "Like the Murmur of the Dove's Song"
- "Spirit of Faith, Come Down"
- "Love, How Deep"

Dramatic Slide Presentation

This slide or video presentation could be shown on Baptism of the Lord Sunday or on Mother's Day. The worship leader or pastor will need to gather pictures of the infants born in the past year, along with other suggested images. In addition, a meditative piece of music can be performed. Possibilities include "Shall We Gather at the River," "Jesus Loves Me," and "Spirit of the Living God." Each text is followed by an image:

"The Spirit of God moved upon the face of the waters." (Genesis 1:2b, KJV)
Image: the surface of a lake

The righteous are planted by streams of living waters. (see Psalm 1:3)
Image: a rushing river

"He leads me beside still waters; he restores my soul." (Psalm 23:2b-3a)
Image: a seashore

"Let justice roll down like waters, and righteousness like an ever-flowing stream." (Amos 5:24)
Image: a waterfall

"No one can enter the kingdom of God without being born of water and Spirit." (John 3:5)
Image: pictures (and names) of those baptized in the past year

"Then he poured water into a basin and began to wash the disciples' feet." (John 13:5)
Image: hands clasped, washing each other

"He will lead them to springs of living water." (Revelation 7:17, NIV)
Image: a scene of a river (different than before)

"Then the angel showed me the river of the water of life." (Revelation 22:1)
Image: a scene of a river (different than before)

Baptize them in the name of the Father and of the Son and of the Holy Spirit. (see Matthew 28:19)
Image: a dove in flight

"I am with you always, to the end of the age." (Matthew 28:20b)
Image: a cross

PASTORAL SITUATIONS

At times, the pastor is asked to offer baptism in response to specific life situations. Persons are not to be re-baptized; God's covenant remains strong despite our inattention to it. We do, however, need ways to access what God has done and is doing for us. The following situations call for expressions of the ritual of baptism (some may also call for rituals of Holy Communion and Anointing with Oil). Prayers and acts of worship are offered for each.

A Health Crisis

Scripture: Luke 17:11-19

Prayer

As we come into your presence
we are cleansed, O God, for you are holy.
Help us to praise God for all signs of wellness.
Raise us into a new life,
In body, mind, and spirit.
May this gift of water renew us,
Cleansing us and making us whole.
Through Jesus Christ, our Healer; Amen.

Nearness to Death

Scripture: Romans 6:1-11

Prayer

Bless your good and faithful servant (*Name*).
As he/she has died and been buried
        with Christ in baptism,
May he/she also rise with Christ in glory.
Remind him/her that the sufferings of this present time
Are not worth comparing with the glory
        that is to be revealed.
Let this water be a sign, a seal
    of your promised spirit,
    and your word that you
        will not leave us comfortless.
Come, Holy Spirit. Come, Lord Jesus. Amen.

Developmental Disabilities

Those with developmental disabilities may be unable to respond verbally, and they may not be rationally responsive to questions. These personal characteristics do not prohibit them from receiving God's grace, or responding to it. The following words might be adapted for particular persons.

(*Name*), you were created in the image of God.
(*Name*), you are a child of God.
(*Name*), Jesus loves you.

Let the person with developmental disabilities touch the water, or take the water and touch his or her forehead.

(*Name*), this water is God's gift to you.
You are baptized, in the name of the Father, the Son, and the Holy Spirit.

—Or—

Remember that you have been baptized, and be thankful.

Entering Military Service

Scripture: Isaiah 43:1-2
Prayer

God of power and might,
Let your strength reside in this your servant.
Watch over him/her.
May this gift of water be a reminder of your
        guidance of your people through the waters
        and of your miracle in calming the storms.
Protect him/her from harm,
And guide him/her in the way of peace;
        through Jesus Christ our Savior; Amen.

CONGREGATIONAL GATHERINGS

For Any Retreat Setting

Scripture: Mark 1:9-11; Matthew 3:13-17
Prayer

God of set-apart places,
We thank you for this setting
In which you seem especially near to us.
We listen closely for your voice,
Speaking to us, calling us by name.
We thank you for the gift of water,
Reminding us of your love for us,
And for the presence of your Spirit,
Poured upon us.
We are your beloved sons and daughters.
Thanks be to God. Amen.

A Meeting for Discernment over Conflict— Baptism and Unity

Greeting
Hymn: "Holy, Holy, Holy"
Confession of Sin

O God, we profess a faith that we do not always live. We hope for a future that we cannot always see. We express love, but we attach limits and conditions. Move us toward a full acceptance of your gifts: faith, hope, and love. Give us hearts to know you. Give us eyes to see you. Give us hands to serve you. In the name of Jesus; Amen.

Words of Assurance (1 John 1:9)

If we confess our sins, [God] who is faithful and just will forgive us our sins and cleanse us from all unrighteousness.

Silence

Scripture Reading: 1 Corinthians 12:1-31

1Now concerning spiritual gifts, brothers and sisters, I do not want you to be uninformed. [2]You know that when you were pagans, you were enticed and led astray to idols that could not speak. [3]Therefore I want you to understand that no one speaking by the Spirit of God ever says "Let Jesus be cursed!" and no one can say "Jesus is Lord" except by the Holy Spirit.

4Now there are varieties of gifts, but the same Spirit; [5]and there are varieties of services, but the same Lord; [6]and there are varieties of activities, but it is the same God who activates all of them in everyone. [7]To each is given the manifestation of the Spirit for the common good. [8]To one is given through the Spirit the utterance of wisdom, and to another the utterance of knowledge according to the same Spirit, [9]to another faith by the same Spirit, to another gifts of healing by the one Spirit, [10]to another the working of miracles, to another prophecy, to another the discernment of spirits, to another various kinds of tongues, to another the interpretation of tongues. [11]All these are activated by one and the same Spirit, who allots to each one individually just as the Spirit chooses.

12For just as the body is one and has many members, and all the members of the body, though many, are one body, so it is with Christ. [13]For in the one Spirit we were all baptized into one body—Jews or Greeks, slaves or free—and we were all made to drink of one Spirit.

14Indeed, the body does not consist of one member but of many. [15]If the foot would say, "Because I am not a hand, I do not belong to the body," that would not make it any less a part of the body. [16]And if the ear would say, "Because I am not an eye, I do not belong to the body," that would not make it any less a part of the body. [17]If the whole body were an eye, where would the hearing be? If the whole body were hearing, where would the sense of smell be? [18]But as it is, God arranged the members in the body, each one of them, as he chose. [19]If all were a single member, where would the body be? [20]As it is, there are many members, yet one body. [21]The eye cannot say to the hand, "I have no need of you," nor again the head to the feet, "I have no need of you." [22]On the contrary, the members of the body that seem to be weaker are indispensable, [23]and those members of the body that we think less honorable we clothe with greater honor, and our less respectable members are treated with greater respect; [24]whereas our more respectable members do not need this. But God has so arranged the body, giving the greater honor to the inferior member, [25]that there may be no dissension within the body, but the members may have the same care for one another. [26]If one member suffers, all suffer together with it; if one member is honored, all rejoice together with it.

27Now you are the body of Christ and individually members of it. [28]And God has appointed in the church first apostles, second prophets, third teachers; then deeds of power, then gifts of healing, forms of assistance, forms of leadership, various kinds of tongues. [29]Are all apostles? Are all prophets? Are all teachers? Do all work miracles? [30]Do all possess gifts of healing? Do all speak in tongues? Do all interpret? [31]But strive for the greater gifts. And I will show you a still more excellent way.

Silence

Testimony

Invite participants, as they are led by God's spirit, to speak words that build up the gathered body of Christ, that confess their own sins, and that contribute to the unity of the one body.

Baptismal Renewal

Invite participants to come forward and touch (or be touched by) the waters of baptism. This act is a sign of the common life that is shared by all the baptized, an identity more significant than our divisions.

Hymn: "Let There Be Peace on Earth"
Peace
Sending Forth

There is one faith, one Lord, one baptism.
Go forth in the peace of God
That transcends every division,
And share your gifts,
So that the body of Jesus Christ may be strengthened
In the power of the Holy Spirit. Amen.

A Mini-Retreat for Commissioned Leaders— Baptism and Service

This retreat is designed for four hours. Adding time for silence, walking, or extended conversation with a spiritual friend can lengthen it.

Gathering and Introductions (20 minutes)
Statement of Theme (5 minutes)

We are called in baptism to be servants of Jesus Christ.

Scripture Reading: Mark 10:35-45 (5 minutes)

35James and John, the sons of Zebedee, came forward to him and said to him, "Teacher, we want you to do for us whatever we ask of you." 36And he said to them, "What is it you want me to do for you?" 37And they said to him, "Grant us to sit, one at your right hand and one at your left, in your glory." 38But Jesus said to them, "You do not know what you are asking. Are you able to drink the cup that I drink, or be baptized with the baptism that I am baptized with?" 39They replied, "We are able." Then Jesus said to them, "The cup that I drink you will drink; and with the baptism with which I am baptized, you will be baptized; 40but to sit at my right hand or at my left is not mine to grant, but it is for those for whom it has been prepared."

41When the ten heard this, they began to be angry with James and John. ⁴²So Jesus called them and said to them, "You know that among the Gentiles those whom they recognize as their rulers lord it over them, and their great ones are tyrants over them. ⁴³But it is not so among you; but whoever wishes to become great among you must be your servant, ⁴⁴and whoever wishes to be first among you must be slave of all. ⁴⁵For the Son of Man came not to be served but to serve, and to give his life a ransom for many."

Silent Reflection (10 minutes)
Hymn: "Spirit of the Living God" (5 minutes)
Small Group Reflection (1 hour and 15 minutes)

- Where do you see individuals serving God in the church? in the community? in the world?
- What is distinctive about service in the name (spirit) of Jesus Christ?
- What is distinctive about the service of your local church?
- Within each small group, one person should read Philippians 2:5-11. Ask the participants to listen to the passage as it is read out loud. Then ask the participants to listen to the passage a second time, noting any word or phrase that resonates with them. Prior to a third reading, ask individuals to listen for an insight into what God is calling them to claim (in terms of identity) or do (in terms of vocation).

Break (15 minutes)
Large Group Gathering (1 hour)

- Brainstorm about the first three small group questions above.
- Have participants report out of their groups.
- What are the common themes and ministries observed?

Teaching (15 minutes)

Have a pastor or teacher give some background to the two biblical passages (Mark 10 and Philippians 2). One resource is Kenneth H. Carter Jr., *The Gifted Pastor* (Abingdon Press, 2001), especially chapter 4, "Spiritual Gifts and Servanthood."

Small Group Reflection on Teaching (15 minutes)
Closing Worship: Service of Baptismal Renewal (15 minutes)

A Service of Covenant Renewal—Baptism and Relationship

This service can be held informally, as a time of spiritual renewal, or in conjunction with a series of renewal or revival services.

Greeting
Hymn: "Blessed Assurance"
Scripture Reading: Romans 6:1-11

1What then are we to say? Should we continue in sin in order that grace may abound? 2By no means! How can we who died to sin go on living in it? 3Do you not know that all of us who have been baptized into Christ Jesus were baptized into his death? 4Therefore we have been buried with him by baptism into death, so that, just as Christ was raised from the dead by the glory of the Father, so we too might walk in newness of life.

5For if we have been united with him in a death like his, we will certainly be united with him in a resurrection like his. 6We know that our old self was crucified with him so that the body of sin might be destroyed, and we might no longer be enslaved to sin. 7For whoever has died is freed from sin. 8But if we have died with Christ, we believe that we will also live with him. 9We know that Christ, being raised from the dead, will never die again; death no longer has dominion over him. 10The death he died, he died to sin, once for all; but the life he lives, he lives to God. 11So you also must consider yourselves dead to sin and alive to God in Christ Jesus.

Confession of Sin

O God, you create us in your image, and yet we rebel against
   your love.
You take our sins upon yourself, in Jesus, and yet we reject
   your grace.
You pour your Spirit upon us, and yet we resist your gifts.
Teach us the way of humility.
Through the power of the cross, have mercy upon us, and for-
   give us.

Words of Assurance (Psalm 51:10)

Create in [us] a clean heart, O God,
   and put a new and right spirit within [us].

Invitation to Baptismal Renewal

Invite participants to come forward and have water placed on
their foreheads, as a remembrance of God's covenant relationship
with them. Invite them to pray at the altar, in a chair, or kneel-
ing, acknowledging that part of life that needs to die, and trust-
ing in God's power to make all things new.

Affirmation of Faith

Invite participants to say the words of a familiar creed.
Examples include:
- The Nicene Creed
- The Apostles' Creed
- A Statement of Faith of The United Church of Canada

For those traditions that do not recite creeds, portions of the
following Scripture passages may be spoken:
- John 14:1-6
- Romans 8:35, 37-39
- Philippians 2:5-11
- Revelation 21:1-5

Sharing the Peace
Sending Forth

Go forth to live in newness of life.
God is faithful, and the One who began a good work in you will
Bring it to completion.
In the name of the Father, the Son, and the Holy Spirit.
    Amen.

PART TWO

SERMONS ON BAPTISM

W e shape the lives of Christians by the actions of the liturgy and also in our teaching and preaching. These ministries, preaching and teaching, interpret the signs and actions that people experience. Sermons and Bible studies clarify the meaning of baptism for adults and youth being baptized and for parents whose children are to be baptized.

The preacher can approach the subject of baptism from a number of perspectives: the baptism of Jesus, the meaning of baptism in the early church, the command of Jesus to make disciples and baptize. Sermons can acknowledge the baptism of a person or extend the invitation to be baptized.

In a message, the preacher can reflect on her or his own baptism, or important baptisms in her or his own journey. In addition, the sermon can lead to reaffirmation of baptismal vows.

The following sermons reflect on Christian baptism in different ways. They will help the reader, hopefully, to engage with these same biblical texts, and his or her own context and life experience. Christian traditions interpret the texts in various ways: issues of immersion in water, or profession preceding baptism, or the need for re-baptism prior to membership in a particular church. These matters are at the discretion of the preacher, and should be shaped by his or her convictions and polity. I have sought in these sermons to focus on the broader significance of baptism, and my intuition is that this is actually the most biblical and effective way to approach the subject.

The sermons are followed by questions for reflection and spiritual exercises. These also are intended to lead the reader into a deeper engagement with the meaning and importance of baptism.

CHILD OF BLESSING, CHILD OF PROMISE

Exodus 2:1-10

The story of the Exodus is situated in an ominous setting. "Now a new king arose over Egypt, who did not know Joseph" (Exodus 1:8). It is a regime change, a new administration is in power, and it is not good. The flow of salvation history that began with Abraham and Sarah and continued in the lives of Isaac and Jacob and Joseph is now interrupted. "A new king arose who did not know Joseph," or his God.

The Israelites are fulfilling the mandate given them in their creation story: "be fruitful and multiply" (Genesis 1:28). They are growing strong, and they are doing the actual work, the actual labor, of the empire, Egypt, building cities like Rameses, for Pharaoh. These manual laborers are growing so large in number and so prosperous that the thought occurs, in the minds of the politicians, "they could become a threat to us, to our way of life." And so the Egyptians become more ruthless to them, they make their lives harder with bitter service. But this, apparently, is not enough. The word comes from Pharaoh, the king who does not know Joseph, or his God: "if you see a Hebrew woman giving birth to a boy, kill him . . . throw him into the Nile."

The Hebrew children are a threat to their way of life. This is not so far from us, if we ponder it. Use your imagination: how, in our world, do we see children not as a blessing, but as a threat to our way of life? Pharaoh saw these people, and the children who would come after them, as a threat. It is an ominous setting.

The focus narrows now, from seeing the larger world to an intimate setting, the birth of a child. A Levite woman, an Israelite, gives birth to a healthy son, and she hides him for three months. Then she puts the baby in a basket—the literal Hebrew word here is found in one other place in the Old Testament—it is the word for *ark*. She puts the baby in an ark, and he sails down the river. She looks on, at a distance. What is going to happen to that baby? If you have children, you have been there. It is called "letting go."

> *When we put them in a weekday school,*
>   *we are letting go.*
> *When we push them into the school bus,*
>   *we are letting go.*
> *When we send them off to camp,*
>   *we are letting go.*
> *When we leave them in the college dorm,*
>   *we are letting go.*
> *When we watch them go off to war,*
>   *we are letting go.*
> *When we see them walking down the aisle,*
>   *we are letting go.*

It is like sailing down the river, floating on the ark, in the midst of the winds and the waves, and we are hoping they make it safely to their destination. Have you ever had that feeling? It *is* about letting go. Moses sails down the river, in the ark. And who should come to bathe at the river but the daughter of Pharaoh? "Oh no," we might think, "This is the end." But there is a surprise. She opens the basket and sees the child. He is crying. And she takes pity on him. She has compassion.

It is a dangerous world for a child. There are dangers we know about—the children and teenagers whose faces appear on our televisions screens—and there are dangers we rarely hear about—children sold into sex slavery in Southeast Asia, children drafted into warfare in Africa. It is a dangerous world for a child. In the middle of the night a man and a little girl enter a restaurant, almost hidden from the sight of the public; he quietly orders their food, and then a waitress, with all kinds of reasons for not getting involved, senses something wrong. She intervenes and the little girl's safety is restored. We know this story.

Pharaoh's daughter senses immediately that this boy is a Hebrew. But then another woman intervenes. The women in this story are the heroes—as they so often are; the women in this story outsmart the men—as they often do. "Should I go and find a woman to nurse the child?" she asks. "Yes," says Pharaoh's daughter. Again, this takes some courage. And so, in a perfect gesture, the sister returns the child to his mother. And Pharaoh's daughter is even going to pay her to do this! The biblical scholars and the rabbis note how cunning the women in this story can be!

So the child grows up, and is later returned to the Pharaoh's daughter, where he is adopted into the royal household. He is given the name Moses because, she said, " 'I drew him out of the water' " (Exodus 2:10b). There are lessons to be learned as we think about this ominous setting and the birth of this child, in the midst of it all.

Lesson Number One

God has a purpose for human history, for our own lives. Think of the decisions of Moses' mother, of his sister. As you read the Gospels of the New Testament, think of Joseph and his dream. God's purpose is often carried out in the decisions that ordinary people make to do the right thing, to do the courageous thing. The small decisions that you make may become a part of God's purpose.

Lesson Number Two

God sometimes uses unlikely people to accomplish God's purposes. Consider the actions of Pharaoh's daughter, or the shepherds and Magi in the New Testament Gospels. Think about your own life and the unlikely people who intervened—the parents of a friend, an aunt or uncle, a coach, a Sunday school teacher, a choir director. God uses unlikely people.

Lesson Number Three

The pharaohs of the world, the Herods of the world, do not always prevail, even though they seem to have the power. It sometimes seems that there is no hope in prevailing against evil, or inhumanity, or greed, or raw political power. And yet watch: God is not content to allow the pharaohs of this world to destroy the world that he has made.

There are lessons with this brief passage. But let's focus for a moment on the child. Moses is a child of blessing, and he is a child of promise. He is blessed. He might have been drowned in the Nile. He might have been killed in some other way by Pharaoh's policy. A less compassionate person might have discovered him. Think about your own life, how it might have been different. Moses is blessed. We know this by the words at the end of the lesson, by the very name given to him: I drew him out of the water. I rescued him. I saved him. This is prevenient grace, the grace that goes before our human response. Salvation is not our work, our effort, lest we should boast, as Paul writes in Ephesians 2. It is a gift of grace. When a child is baptized, she or he is touched by these very same waters, and reminded that she or he is a part of God's purpose, God's plan.

Moses is also a child of promise. He is rescued, saved for a purpose. This is sanctifying grace, the grace that follows our salvation, that completes our salvation. We are saved for a purpose. Why was Moses drawn out of the water? Moses is going to lead his people to freedom. Sometimes, as Christians, we think that if we have been baptized or accepted Christ or been confirmed, this is some kind of revered status, maybe one that makes us better than other people. One of my favorite lines of late was spoken about a prominent politician: he was born on third base and he thinks he hit a triple!

We forget that it is all grace. Think about the people who saw you through the eyes of compassion, who took care of your needs, who kept you from falling in over your head. And sometimes, once we have become Christians, once we have been adopted into the royal household, we think *that's it*, the equation is completed.

Every Christian is a child of blessing and a child of promise. The blessing is what God has done for us. The promise is what God wants to do through us. The blessing is where we have been. The promise is where we are going. The blessing is what we receive. The promise is what we are asked to give. The blessing is that grace has brought us safe thus far. The promise is that grace will lead us home.

It is an ominous world, a dangerous world to be a child. If leaders can crush the people, they often do. Pharaoh is very much alive. And perhaps we wonder: who will save us? Perhaps a new Moses is being born, even now.

> *Born thy people to deliver*
> *Born a child and yet a king*
> *Born to reign in us forever*
> *Now thy gracious kingdom bring*
> *Come thou long expected Jesus*
> *Born to set thy people free.*
> —*"Come Thou Long Expected Jesus" by Charles Wesley*

Come, Lord Jesus, child of blessing, child of promise. Amen.

For Spiritual Reflection and Further Learning

- Read the poem by Madeleine L'Engle entitled "The Risk of Birth, Christmas, 1973," which is included in *The Weather of the Heart*.
- Read a commentary on the first two chapters of the book of Exodus.
- Look for connections between the books of Genesis and Exodus.

HIS BAPTISM AND OURS

Matthew 3:13-17

They don't exactly meet by accident. The place is important, the wilderness through which the Jordan River runs. Two devout Jews encounter each other. They're there for the same reason. They knew the family story: how God had set their people free from slavery, how he had brought them through the waters, how they had wandered in the wilderness as far as Moses could take them, and then Joshua had led them into the Promised Land.

Now the people are enslaved again, this time by the Romans, and they are awaiting a new Moses. Some of them cluster around a man named John, who stands near the river, plunging people into it, reminding them that God is still in the business of saving people.

Even now, God is in the business of saving people. The water is a symbol of all of that, the Exodus, the journey from slavery to freedom, from the old life to the new. People come from long distances to remember this story, to step into these waters. Jesus is one of them.

And here is the meeting that is not by accident. It was bound to happen. Jesus comes from the Galilee to be baptized by John. But something here is not quite right: we might call it *the protocol*. "I need to be baptized by you," John says. Now John has a strong and healthy ego; he is not a shrinking violet, but he knows the reality of the situation. "I need to be baptized by you," he says. "You're coming to me?"

John resists. But Jesus makes it clear. Let it be so, go ahead, baptize me to fulfill all righteousness. It is the right thing to do.

Rituals were important in the time of Jesus. For Jews, the great ritual was circumcision. Eight days after his birth, Jesus was circumcised in the temple, taken there by Joseph and Mary. Simeon and Anna were there to give thanks for the fulfillment of prophecy. For Gentiles who wanted to become Jews, a ritual baptism was required. The Qumran community, where the Dead Sea Scrolls were found, required water baptism. John the Baptist went out in the wilderness, to the Jordan, to baptize.

It was an important ritual. Later, in the history of Christianity, it would become one of the two sacraments shared by most Christian denominations. A sacrament, by definition, is an outward and visible sign of an inward and spiritual grace. The other sacrament, for most Christians, is Holy Communion. Through baptism, we become a part of the people of God, the body of Christ. We become God's adopted children. And through Holy Communion, we are nourished, sustained, fed. As baptism points backward to the Exodus, Holy Communion also has its roots in the Passover. And so Jesus did these two things: he was baptized; he shared a Passover meal with his disciples. Again, not by accident.

Jesus could easily have said, *"Why should I be baptized?"* And we might well ask the same question. He had no imperfection, no sin, no need to be washed. He was the Son of God. And yet he did it to fulfill all righteousness. The baptism of Jesus was the right thing to do, for us, for our sake.

This question parallels another one: why do *we* participate in rituals? Can't we get by without them? I've heard at least one evangelist say, "All the water in the world won't save you." Maybe so, but that's beside the point: Jesus was baptized. Jesus participated in the ritual. A few years ago, the popular question was, "What would Jesus do?" Well, Jesus' life was shaped by rituals.

And so are our lives. If we are going to taste the inward and spiritual grace, we must be able to recognize the outward and visible sign. And so we put ourselves in a place, sometimes by habit, sometimes by desire, sometimes because it has become a ritual. And in that place *something good happens*. The outward and visible sign is always *connected* to the inward and spiritual grace.

So Jesus is baptized. Matthew says he came up from the water. Close readers of Scripture will recognize that this looks a lot like baptism by immersion. Students of geography will argue that many portions of the Jordan River are very shallow. We know from the New Testament that adults were baptized, and we also know that children and whole families were baptized (see Acts 16). Jesus is baptized and amazing things happen: the heavens open, a dove descends, a voice speaks. The light shines upon him;

he is aware that he is not alone—the Spirit is there—and there is a word: "You are my son, my beloved, I am pleased with you."

And the story moves on from there.

I wanted to spend some time with the baptism of Jesus for a simple reason—it is important that we connect our baptisms to his. Like Jesus, we are a part of a larger story, and here the baptism of infants has meaning. Many of us were baptized at a very young age—this is common among Methodists, Lutherans, Presbyterians, Episcopalians, Catholics, and Orthodox. In some traditions, you were carried to the front of an altar, a pastor asked the question, "What name is given this child?" and someone spoke your name. And then you were baptized.

Or perhaps your son or daughter was baptized. If it was your baptism, you may not remember much about it and maybe it seems like an empty exercise. But other people can help us with memory, and rituals are important. When you were baptized, you became a part of a larger story, and that is why we remember the salvation history each time we baptize someone: the waters of creation, crossing the Jordan, Mary's womb, Jesus' baptism, his commandment to go and make disciples and to baptize them.

We are a part of a larger story. One of my favorite movies of the past few years was *Big Fish*. It was the story of a son trying to learn about his dying father by getting him to retell the stories of his life. The father's stories are pretty amazing—as a baby, he went shooting out of his mother's womb down the hallway. At eight, he was bedridden for three years. To pass the time he read through the encyclopedia and came to the reference to goldfish: "If goldfish are kept in a small bowl, they will remain small. With more space, the fish can double, triple or quadruple in size." He decided that he needed to do bigger things in this life: he became a star athlete, a science fair winner, and a hero when he rescued a dog from a burning building. He was presented the keys to a small town for convincing a giant, seen as a monster by many, to leave town with him. He went into the world, because he was unwilling to be a "big fish in a small pond." Without giving away the ending, I can say it was a baptism, and he was carried back into the waters and released.

The son gradually realizes that this adventure might in fact be true. We need a story that is larger than our own stories. In *Big Fish*, the son listens to the larger story of his father's life, for only then can he make sense of his own story. It helps to know the larger story; it helps to know our own stories. I will tell you a portion of mine. I grew up in the church, off and on, in and out. Mostly our family was present in church—my mother, my grandfather, my great-grandmother, aunts and cousins, brother and sister. We were a part of the Baptist church, later the Methodist church, back to the Baptist church, then again the Methodist church. I don't come down too hard on people who change churches or flow among them; this was our family history.

As a teenager I became aware that I had never been baptized. And so one evening I talked with the pastor about it. A couple of weeks later I was baptized. It felt great.

Many years later I was talking with someone in our family, and he mentioned that when I was a very small infant, all of our family went down to Sanford, Florida, where my great-grandfather, a Congregational minister, lived. And he had baptized me that Sunday.

Of course, I never knew this. I had imagined that baptism was all about my struggle, my decision, my faith. And yet I could look back and see that it was just as much the result of being in a family that took faith seriously, and that offered grace before I was aware of it. My story was a part of a larger story.

And that's important for us to know too. Sometimes we experience something, or we receive a gift, and years later it means something to us. The richness of the rituals points to future experiences of God's grace. Do we really know what we are getting into when we get married? Or when we have a child? Or when we join a church? The answer, if we are honest, is probably "no." But these are rituals that expose us to God's love, to God's blessing, to God's community.

I am not so concerned if you don't remember your experience of baptism, or if it didn't mean that much to you then. I want it to mean something to you now. And here the Scripture helps us. Baptism, in its origin, had to do with being made clean. And the importance of baptism has to do with our universal need to be made clean. From the perspective of God, after the fallenness of creation, we are all living in a moral sewer. All have sinned and fall short of the glory of God, Paul writes in Romans 3:23.

When I was in divinity school, a popular book about the church, by Daniel Zeluff, was entitled *There's Algae in the Baptismal "Fount."* The words remind us of a church and a culture where the rituals are forgotten, where we see no need for them. No one needs to be baptized because no one needs to be cleansed; we're really good people, right? And if we needed to get our act together, we would get a professional to help us do it.

Of course, we do have a common need for cleansing. Throughout history we have devised many ways to distinguish between Christians—elders and deacons, priests and bishops, clergy and laity—but at the core we share this one experience: we have been baptized.

And the good news of the Gospel is that Jesus shares this with us. He stands with us and for us and beside us. He does it to fulfill all righteousness.

This has a meaning for us as a church. Sometimes we think we exist as the church in order to make other people clean, as if the church is clean and the world is unclean.

Where did we get this idea? Maybe it comes from the experience many of us had as children. On Sundays, we got all *cleaned up* and we went to church. There was something good about that—it showed reverence to God. But psychologically, there was something wrong—we don't come to church because we are clean. We come to church because we are unclean. We want to be in the place where Jesus can touch us and cleanse us and make us new.

We have a common need for grace. We have a common need to be clean. We have a common need for the Holy Spirit to descend upon us. We have a common need to hear the word of blessing, "You are my son; you are my daughter, and I am pleased with you."

Remember that you have been baptized. Remember, when you hear those words, and are invited to come forward to touch the waters of baptism, or have a pastor make the sign of the cross on your forehead with the water.

Remember that you have been baptized, and be thankful. You are a part of something that is larger than you are. It is the adventure of the baptismal life. You are beginning to claim something that was done for you long ago. You are being made clean, even now. And after you have been blessed and cleansed, you are released into the world to tell the story of Jesus and his love.

Remember your baptism, and be thankful!

In the name of the Father, the Son,
and the Holy Spirit. Amen.

For Spiritual Reflection and Further Learning
- Watch the film *Big Fish*, based on the novel by Daniel Wallace.
- Write a narrative about your own baptism.
- Compare the accounts of Jesus' baptism in Matthew 3, Mark 1, and Luke 3.

I HAVE CALLED YOU BY NAME

Isaiah 43:1-7

In a world of many gods and multiple creation stories, this one God—the God of Abraham, Isaac, and Jacob—makes a claim about what is true: "I created you, I formed you." And then, in orthodox Christian fashion, creation moves to history, Genesis to Exodus.

The prophet Isaiah states the claim in verse 1 of chapter 43: "I have redeemed you [from slavery]; I have called you by name [Israel], you are mine."

"You only have I known of all the families of the earth," the Lord spoke through a later prophet, Amos (3:2).

Isaiah's statement of the claim continues in 43:2-3:

When you pass through the waters
[on the way to the Promised Land],
    I will be with you . . .
When you walk through fire [when your temple is destroyed by the
pagan outsiders] you shall not be burned,
    and the flame shall not consume you.
For I am the LORD *your God,*
    the Holy One of Israel, your Savior.

As the old refrain from "Blessed Assurance" has it: "This is my story, this is my song."

Today, we come to *remember* our story, to *reclaim* our story, to *tell* our story. We give thanks that God created this church, that God formed this church. We honor those who have formed us, teachers and preachers and witnesses and friends and servants and musicians, our parents and grandparents in the faith. It is good to remember and to give thanks.

My grandmother had as much to do as any human being with my coming to accept the Christian faith. She did this in a quiet, persistent way. She did this through her words and her cooking— I can almost taste, twenty years later, her roast beef marinated in Coca-Cola from one of those small bottles. She did this in letters that she continued to write to me throughout her life, even though her formal education was completed prior to finishing high school. At her memorial service I was asked to give a family witness; I stood to speak and I was beginning and I found that I could go no further, I could say no more . . .

Sometimes we don't have the words, but that doesn't keep us from remembering. When we remember our baptism, we reclaim a heritage that is ours, we sift the soil in which we have been planted. The church that I serve has a large AA community, and one night as I was walking through the hall a woman—I didn't know her—was looking at the picture of the old church building, no longer standing, and she said, "You ought to make this picture more prominent—a lot of people got sober in that building."

Some of our heritage is in pictures, some of our heritage is living, and it is, especially in worship, the *people* who are gathered.

These are people who could make some claim upon the words of the Lord, to us, about our spiritual lives, "I created you, I formed you." Disciples are made, not born. This is another way of saying we are a part of a tradition here, one that has spanned many years. As Jaroslav Pelikan has said: "Tradition is the living faith of the dead; traditionalism is the dead faith of the living" (*The Christian Tradition: A History of the Development of Doctrine:* vol. 1 of 5: *The Emergence of the Catholic Tradition (100-600),* [Chicago: The University of Chicago Press, 1971], 9).

I created you; I formed you. I have redeemed you.
I have called you by name.

This is the personal meaning of the story, as the refrain goes, "This is my story, this is my song." The great work of God in the creation of all that is, seen and unseen, has to do with the work that God is also doing in you and in me.

I have called you by name. You are mine. You have a
purpose. You have a destiny. You have a calling.

Names shape our identity. Jacob wrestles with the angel all night long, and in the process he becomes a new person, he is given a new name: Israel. Jesus stands in the waters of the Jordan River, and the light shines above him and the dove lands upon him and the voice speaks, and says, "You are my son, you are my beloved, I am pleased with you." Maybe you can remember carrying a son or daughter to the waters of baptism in your church, and a pastor asked the question, "What name is given this child?" and you spoke the name. Maybe you are saying it now, silently, under your breath.

I have called you by name—Israel, Christ.

On one of my journeys to Israel, I was standing in the Jordan River. We were an interracial group of Jews and Christians and the Jews were watching as the Christians were positioned on the edge of the water. I was standing with a good friend, an African American pastor in the Baptist tradition. He said, "Ken, remember your baptism and be thankful." Then he dunked me under the water. Then, he looked at me and said, "I've always wanted to do that to a Methodist!"

Of course, our baptisms connect us in ways that transcend denominations.

Our baptisms connect us with these—the history of Israel, the presence of the beloved Son, Jesus, the church universal— because God always extends love to us through particular people and God always makes himself known to us in particular places. It is not an abstraction. It is here, now. This church. This place. These people. You.

"I have called you by name. You are mine. When you pass through the waters, I will be with you. When you walk through the fire, you shall not be burned, the flames will not consume you."

Jesus stands in these waters with us. He embodies the passage of Israel from slavery to freedom. He takes our sin upon himself. He stands with us, intercedes for us. He takes our place. All of the sin of human history is washed away in those cleansing waters.

The church, at its best, remembers this truth. Storms come in the life of the church. Fires rage around the church. Sometimes the church is not only the victim of life's adversities; sometimes it is part of the problem. The story is told of Bishop Gerald Kennedy, of the twentieth-century Methodist Church, that he used to rewrite hymns when he became bored at Council of Bishops' meetings. One he wrote survives:

> *"Like a mighty tortoise, moves the church of God.*
> *Brethren we are treading where we've always trod!"*

The church is an earthen vessel (2 Corinthians 4).

A minister friend told of a devout woman who had been a lifelong member of one of the largest churches of our denomination. This very visible church had been at the center of a storm, a scandal, for almost two years. The beloved and personally charismatic pastor was charged and convicted of the near murder of his wife. The television cameras and media were a constant presence, the newspaper reports ongoing. It was chaos. Each week this devout woman took her same place in the same pew; she remained faithful. My friend asked her, "How do you keep going, how can you worship, how can you keep your faith?" She responded, "Each week I come into this place and I open the hymnal to the page where it is written, 'The church is of God, and will be preserved until the end of time.'"

"When you pass through the waters, I will be with you . . . when you walk through fire you shall not be burned, and the flame shall not consume you" (Isaiah 43:2). The church endures adversity, but the grace of God "has brought us safe thus far, and grace will lead us home" ("Amazing Grace"). God stands with us in the waters of baptism.

- Maybe you are in church, ready for a new beginning in life, a new start. God says, "I created you, I formed you." When you are touched by the waters of baptism, the cleansing of your soul is the miraculous work of the Lord. Imagine the Voice speaking to you, and saying, "You are my son, you are my daughter, I am pleased with you."
- Maybe you have lost a sense of purpose and direction in life. God says, "I have called you by name, you are mine." When you are touched by the waters of baptism, you become a part of a larger purpose: the history of Israel, and the life and death and resurrection of Jesus. Imagine that God is calling you, by name, you, for some purpose.
- Maybe you are in the midst of some adversity; you are in trouble. When you are touched by the waters of baptism, a calming presence will come upon you. Imagine a hand being laid upon you and a Voice saying, "You are not alone; I will be with you."

God is not finished with us yet. "From the past will come the future," Natalie Sleeth's "Hymn of Promise" reminds us.

Hear the word of the Lord

> I created you
> I formed you
> When you pass through the waters,
>   I will be with you.
> When you walk through the flames,
>   they will not consume you.
> I have called you by name.

For Spiritual Reflection and Further Learning

- Can you recall a time of adversity in your own life, when you felt as if you were "passing through the waters" or "walking through the fire"?
- Reflect on what about your Christian tradition is life-giving, and what is not.
- Listen to "Be Not Afraid," as recorded by the Saint Louis Jesuits on *Earthen Vessels*. Or thumb through a hymnal and locate a hymn that speaks of God's watch and care for you.

New Birth: Why Baptism Matters

Galatians 3:23-29

I don't watch a great deal of television, although there certainly seems to be something there for everyone: whether you want to watch a baseball game being played today or one that took place ten years ago, or three or four or five guys talk or argue about sports . . . I could go on.

In scanning the television stations, I have noticed a prominent theme of late—our desire for transformation, change, a makeover. In some shows you leave, and when you return your home has been decorated in a new way. Or you travel someplace, like New York City, and you become a new person: new hair, a new wardrobe. Or five guys come in and they teach you a new way to cook, and they decorate, and they get rid of all of your old stuff. Or, more drastically, a team of surgeons, along with a very attractive model/spokesperson, consults with you and convinces you that you need a new body and a new face.

It is all about makeover, transformation, change. Of course, the networks are tapping into something very powerful: the impulse to shed our skin, to experience a metamorphosis from an ugly duckling to a swan, from a caterpillar to a butterfly.

This impulse is deep within Christians as well; the way we talk about makeover, transformation, change, and new life is baptism. In Galatians 3, Paul speaks of an old way of life, under the custodian, the disciplinarian, the pedagogy of the law; a law that we could not keep or live up to or fulfill. The law held this place over us until Christ came, Paul tells the Galatians. In Christ we become children of God. We are not speaking of natural childbirth, of the mark of circumcision, or of any kind of ethnic heritage. We are children of God through faith.

This faith is expressed in baptism; we are baptized *into* Christ—into the body—and we "put on Christ." The image is unmistakable—as if we are receiving a new wardrobe. And because we have put on Christ, we are made over, we are transformed, we are changed. The old camp song I learned in the mountains of western North Carolina said it well:

The best thing in my life I ever did do,
Was take off the old robe and put on the new.

Baptism is a visual symbol of the power of transformation. It is God's gift, God's work, God's act. Baptism also gives us a different way of perceiving ourselves. In these programs on television, the person leaves, and they return, and maybe they see a room or two, in their homes, and everything is different, and the camera records their amazement. Or perhaps someone leaves, and they return to see their friends and family, who cannot believe she is the same person. Or the surgically improved individual simply looks into a mirror and is overwhelmed. It is all about getting used to the change.

In the New Testament church, the converts needed some reassurance that they were worthy of God's gift, worthy of love. And so, Paul says to the Galatians, and to us, "you are all children of God" (3:26). Peter, in his first letter, says, "you are . . . royal" (2:9). You have a new identity. You belong to God.

A good friend of ours had her first child this spring, a boy. We saw him last week, for the first time. As I picked him up, I was amazed, first, at how light he seemed, our children having grown almost to adulthood. I smiled at him, made some goofy noises— I'll spare you those—and he looked at me as if he were going through some kind of internal biochemical reaction.

Then Susan, his mother, took him back, and said his name, and a huge smile came across his face. He knew the one to whom he belonged.

Do we know that? Do we know that we belong to God? That is a transforming truth. The primary identifying feature about you is not where you live or how you vote or how much money you have or where you came from or who your father is or even your gender or your race. You are a child of God, through faith, in baptism.

In baptism, we are marked and claimed. In baptism, we are told that we belong. And of course, we sometimes forget that we belong. People join churches with the best of intentions, and they make promises to support the congregation with their prayers, presence, gifts, and service. "This is what I will do; this is who we will be." And sometimes they—sometimes we—forget. In baptism we are assured that we are children of God, but maybe the world tells us that we have failed, fallen short, missed the mark, and we are ignored or downsized or cut off or shut out, and it is easy to forget that we are children of God.

I have a friend who can remember times when he would go out, as a teenager, sometimes with groups, sometimes on dates, and his mother or his father would say to him, as he raced toward the door, "Remember who you are!"

We will often repeat the phrase, "Remember your baptism, and be thankful." Remember that you are a child of God, and you will always be a child of God, and nothing that you do can ever change that. You may wander away into some far country, but God will be waiting for you.

And so, I invite you to "remember your baptism, and be thankful." It helps us to access the grace that God wants to give us. And it helps us to see one another in a new way.

> There is no longer Jew or Greek, there is no longer slave or free, there is no longer male and female; for all of you are one in Christ Jesus. (Galatians 3:28)

A common rabbinic prayer, prayed by a male religious leader, went like this:

> I thank you God,
> that I was not born a Gentile,
> that I was not born a woman,
> that I was not born a dog.

That prayer seems shocking to us, and yet, we all make distinctions about each other. But in Christ, there is neither Jew nor Greek, slave nor free, male nor female. You are all one in Christ Jesus. What we share in common—our identity in Jesus Christ—is more significant than all of our differences.

Which is another way of saying, we all belong. Baptism is about transformation; we can be changed. Baptism is about identity; we belong. And baptism is a lifelong process; we live into the changes. When we are watching television, it all happens so quickly, and yet real change, real transformation is different. We are becoming new creatures. We are being changed.

On television, it happens in an instant. But in reality, the change, the makeover, the transformation may take our entire lives.

So stay tuned. A sacrament is an outward and visible sign of an inward and spiritual grace. The change, the makeover, the transformation that matters is one that begins on the inside, what John Wesley called the "circumcision of the heart," what Jesus pointed to in so many of the teachings of the Sermon on the Mount.

The outward and visible sign is the water: washing over us. The inward and spiritual grace is the acceptance, the unconditional love, the fount of every blessing, always a gift, a moment that extends into a lifetime, like "streams of mercy, never ceasing, [that] call for [our] songs of loudest praise" (from "Come, Thou Fount of Every Blessing" by Robert Robinson).

At times we will remember who we are, and at times we will forget. And yet, God is not finished with us . . . God will not give up on us. Our lives, our priorities, are being rearranged. Welcome to the family, God says . . . let's get you cleaned up!

And so we place ourselves in God's hands, and we allow the waters to cleanse us, and our hearts are tuned to sing God's grace, and we see ourselves, and each other, for who we really are. We remember that we are baptized. We hear a voice calling our name, and if we are listening, a huge smile comes across our faces. We are children of God!

For Spiritual Reflection and Further Learning

- Locate, read, and reflect on the hymn, "Come Thou Fount of Every Blessing" (*The United Methodist Hymnal* [Nashville: The United Methodist Publishing House, 1989], 400).
- Reflect on an experience of transformation in your own spiritual journey.
- What is the dark side of our culture's fascination with newness and perfection? What response can we offer as baptized Christians?
- Read a commentary on Galatians 3. What were the issues underlying Paul's teaching about our human distinctions alongside oneness in Christ?

I Am With You
(You're on Your Own)

Baptism of the Lord Sunday—Isaiah 43:1-7

The good news of God, as we enter into a new year, is expressed in four words: "I am with you." I invite you to say these words with me: **"I am with you."**

"Do not fear," says the Lord to Israel and to us, "I am with you. I have created you. I have redeemed you. I have called you by name. You are mine. When you pass through the waters, I will be with you."

As we begin a new year, this is about the best news we can hear. It is not my word. It is the word of the Lord, "I am with you."

The gospel can be summed up in a few simple words. I am still working on selecting these words. Maybe you can help me.

The first three essential words were: **"He is risen."**

The next four essential words were: **"The Word became flesh."**

Now there are four more essential words: **"I am with you."**

These are four of the most important words we can hear, or say. Say those words to the person nearest you. **"I am with you."**

That God says them to us, about us, is utterly amazing: "I am with you."

At Christmas we discover this truth. His name shall be called Emmanuel, which means, God with us; which is another way of saying, I am with you.

Now the world says something very different to us. The world says, "You're on your own."

Do you have a problem with the product we've just sold you? "You're on your own."

Are you having a bad day emotionally? "You're on your own."

Having trouble figuring out that math problem at school? "You're on your own."

Now it should not surprise us that the word that the world

speaks to us is so at odds with the word of God. But which word seems more real, more true to us: "I am with you," or "you're on your own"?

To answer that question we need rituals, things to do that make the words come alive, things people have been doing for a long time, years, centuries, millennia.

First, we need to remember that we have been baptized. And when we remember that we have been baptized, we remember that Jesus stands with us in our baptism. He stands with us in the waters of the Jordan River.

We are sinners. Let's say that together: **"We are sinners."**

We are all sinners. We are all living in sin.

And Jesus comes along and says, "I see you living in sin." And you know what Jesus could have said? He could have said, "You're on your own."

But you know what? He said something different. Instead, he said, "I am with you."

Can you believe that? He stands in the waters of baptism with us. He says, "I am with you."

Second, we need to eat this meal with Jesus. And when we eat this meal with Jesus, we remember that he ate with sinners.

Jesus saw us. He was eating at the table with his friends. Maybe we were all alone, sitting at the bar. Remember, we're sinners. And did Jesus say, "You, over there, you're on your own"?

No, instead, he said, "I want to share this meal with you." Which was his way of saying, "I am with you."

He stands in the waters of baptism with us.

He sits at the table and eats with us.

And third, he makes a promise with us.

Jesus is the new covenant. He says, even if we have broken the promise, even if we have rebelled against the law, even if we have resisted grace . . . we can never get so far away from God that he says, "You're on your own."

The word of God is always, "I am with you."

And so we have this opportunity, once again.

To touch the waters, once again,

> to remember that you have been baptized and be
> thankful;
> To eat the bread and drink from the cup,
> to take within ourselves the very presence
> of the living Lord;
> To make the promise in a new year,
> on this first Sunday.
> It is our opportunity to say these words
> back to God: "God, I am with you."

I want you to say those words out loud: **"God, I am with you."**
The world speaks a lie: "You're on your own." God speaks truth: "I am with you."

The words "I am with you" create community.

The words "I am with you" create relationship.

The words "I am with you" create covenant.

The words "I am with you" create communion.

This morning, brothers and sisters, the good news is for all of us. The world says, "You're on your own." God says, "I am with you." Listen again to the prophet Isaiah (43:1-7):

> *Do not fear, for I have redeemed you;*
> *I have called you by name,*
> *you are mine.*
> *When you pass through the waters,*
> *I will be with you;*
> *and through the rivers, they*
> *shall not overwhelm you;*
> *when you walk through fire you*
> *shall not be burned,*
> *and the flame shall not consume you.*
> *For I am the* LORD *your God,*
> *the Holy One of Israel, your Savior.*
> *. . . . .*
> *. . . you are precious in my sight,*
> *and honored, and I love you. . . .*
> *Do not fear, for I am with you.*

Amen.

For Spiritual Reflection and Further Learning

- Say the words of this prayer, an adaptation of "A Covenant Prayer in the Wesleyan Tradition":

I give myself completely to you, God.
Assign me to my place in your creation.
Let me suffer for you. Give me the work
        you would have me do.
Give me many tasks, or have me step aside
        while you call others.
Put me forward or humble me. Give me riches
        or let me live in poverty.
I freely give all that I am and all that I have to you.
And now, Holy God—Father, Son and Holy Spirit—
You are mine and I am yours. So be it.
May this covenant made on earth continue
        for all eternity. Amen.

- How, in a service of worship, can you connect baptism and Holy Communion?
- How have you experienced the reality of these two different sayings, "I am with you" and "You're on your own"?

THROUGH THE DEEP WATERS

Matthew 3:13-17

At the conclusion of this service we will ask you to remember your baptisms. And so this week I have been remembering baptisms—the baptisms of our children. Our older daughter was baptized at Lake Junaluska. I was serving four churches at the time, and I didn't quite know how to have the baptism at one church. I didn't want to baptize her four times—that would be a little much. Junaluska was about halfway between my wife's family in North Carolina and my family in Georgia. The baptism was scheduled for one in the afternoon in the Memorial Chapel right beside the lake. The Bishop was going to baptize her. He finally arrived. We had a brief service. Somehow we forgot to include the music that our friend, an organist, had chosen. Afterward, the Bishop lost his robe or it was stolen (who would want a Bishop's robe?). For years, and he was our Bishop for twelve years, he would see me and remember the baptism, and then he would say, "Yeah, I lost my robe that day."

Our younger daughter was baptized at a church I was serving a few years later. Our best friend from divinity school came from Florida to perform the service. We set the date. At the last minute I discovered there would be another baptism in the same service. I had mixed feelings for a while—hey, this was supposed to be our service!—and yet they were friends too, and it was their church too, and so both children were baptized, one after another. I worked with my friend, the director of music, on a baptismal piece I wanted the choir to do—the same piece that had been omitted from the previous baptism—and this time the music director forgot it! I guess it wasn't meant to be.

I remember both of those baptisms! I remember other baptisms. I have baptized teenagers by immersion, climbing into the big wader boots, and going down into the tank. I remember holding a child who had Tay-Sachs disease, who lived only a year or two longer, and baptizing him. I remember standing in the chilly and cold waters of the River Jordan one spring, and going under, remembering my baptism as a Baptist pastor friend dunked me under!

There are also wonderful stories about baptisms. A pastor friend in another state was baptizing a little boy, who might have been two years old. The boy was holding his mother's hand, and then, the next moment, he had broken away and he ran down the side of the sanctuary, his parents chasing after him!

It is good to remember our baptisms. We do that first by remembering that Jesus was baptized. It is good to pay close attention to the scripture, Matthew 3:13-17. Jesus comes to the Galilee for this specific purpose. It is not an accident. John tries to resist. He is aware of the superiority of Jesus. Jesus corrects him. He wants to be baptized by John to fulfill all righteousness. Fulfillment is important. This baptism, like our baptisms, is part of a larger story. We didn't invent this. Neither did Jesus. His life is the fulfillment of something. He is there to fulfill all righteousness. He is obedient to the will of God in his life and mission.

When a child is baptized, there is also the anticipation of fulfillment: that the faith will be passed to the next generation, that the mighty acts of God will continue in the future to bless as they have in the past. And there is obedience. The parents make promises to God; the congregation also makes promises to the family.

Jesus is baptized and comes out of the water. The heavens open. God is revealing himself and the Spirit of God descends like a dove and lights on him. Then comes the voice of God: "This is my Son, the Beloved, I am pleased with him."

Notice what is happening: there is a new creation, the dove, symbolic of the Holy Spirit, moving over the waters. In Matthew 1:1, Jesus is announced: the son of David, the son of Abraham. Now in Matthew 3:17, the announcement is completed: the Son of God.

At the beginning of Matthew, the Father, the Son, and the Holy Spirit are present in the baptism. At the end of Matthew's Gospel, in the Great Commission, we are instructed to baptize in the name of the Father, the Son, and the Holy Spirit. And so we baptize in the Trinity, remembering this scripture: the dove lighting on him, the voice speaking to him, Father, Son, Holy Spirit.

This is a rich moment, extending back in time to the beginning of creation, gathering together all of the prophetic visions—Ezekiel saw the heavens opening—and anticipating a future that Jesus would embrace through the obedience that ended on a cross at Golgotha. But it was all there, in the baptism, as he stood in the Jordan.

We can only remember our baptisms if we remember the baptism of Jesus. Our baptisms only make sense if we see them in that way. He became like us in his baptism so that we might become like him. In baptism he did not become something that he was not already. He was already Emmanuel. He was already the object of the wise men's worship. He was already the Messiah. But in baptism his obedience became clear. He was there to fulfill all righteousness.

That is at the heart of our baptisms too: obedience. So we ask the question: "Do you renounce the spiritual forces of wickedness?"

There was a sense in the early church that turning to Jesus meant turning away from other things. The problem with American Christianity is that liberals have their list of sins that would be defined as wicked and conservatives have their list of sins that would be defined as wicked, and each thinks the other is captive to the spiritual forces of wickedness. There are some things we must turn from in order to turn to Jesus.

We ask, "Do you accept the freedom and power God gives you to resist evil, injustice and oppression in whatever forms they present themselves?" Jesus Christ purchased our freedom, and we claim it in our baptism. We turn away from something in order to turn to something greater. We let go of something in order to receive something more.

We ask, "Do you confess Jesus Christ as your Savior, put your whole trust in his grace, and promise to serve him as your Lord?" One of my favorite movies is *Tender Mercies*, starring Robert Duvall. He was a musician, drifting in the middle of nowhere, in Texas, when he meets a woman with a small boy, a young widow who owns a small gas station. They fall in love, they get married, and his life is saved. And in a memorable scene in the movie, he is baptized. At the same time the boy is also baptized. They are riding back from the service. As I recall the dialogue, the boy turns to him and says,

"Well, we've done it, Mac. We're baptized."

"Yeah we are," Mac responds.

Sonny continues: "Everybody said I was going to feel like a changed person. I guess I do feel a little different, but I don't feel a whole lot different. Do you?"

Mac responds, "Not yet."

"You don't look different," Sonny says as he looks at Mac. "Do you think I look any different?"

Mac only answers with another, "Not yet."

And yet there is a joy in their faces. God has begun to do something in their lives. Baptism is a reminder to each of us that this is all about a Savior and his grace. And that is a reminder to each of us that we need cleansing, washing, renewing. We're not just good and upstanding people here who can make it on our own. We need to be washed. We need to be cleansed. We need to be saved.

The liturgy continues: "Do you confess Jesus Christ as your Savior, put your whole trust in his grace, and promise to serve him as your Lord, in union with the church which Christ has opened to people of all ages, nations and races?"

I was thinking this week of a very different movie, *Romero*. It is the story of the martyred Archbishop Oscar Romero of El Salvador. He has a relationship with a wealthy family—they had often had dinner together, but they began to have differences, especially about the lives of the poor in their country. Arista, the wife, comes to schedule a baptism with the archbishop. He says that's fine but that his schedule won't permit it unless some of the other children are included for baptism. She refuses, stating that her child will not be baptized with the *Indian* children! And so she rejects the grace of God, because it is for all people.

The waters are for all of us. Not for some of us, all of us. When I was a child, our family would go to Callaway Gardens, a large man-made lake below Atlanta. It was great. It had a beach. It had a concession stand. It had a circus. And in the heat of the summer it was a welcome relief from the South Georgia heat. I remember, as clearly as if it happened yesterday, large buses arriving at Callaway Gardens. Black children, boys and girls, got out of those buses and streamed into the lake with us. This was in the mid-1960s. And I remember the comments that I heard, that I won't repeat. Most of us knew the Bible. We knew the old hymns about being washed in the blood of the Lamb. But we were rejecting the grace of God. We missed the point that the church of Jesus Christ is "open to people of all ages, nations, and races."

The waters that wash us are deep, deep enough to cleanse us from all of our sin, all of our prejudices, all of our stereotypes, all of our wounds, all of our rebellion against God, all of our rejection of grace. When you touch the waters you become a part of a great stream, a great history of Moses and Miriam, Jesus and

Mary, Paul and Peter, Oscar Romero and Mother Teresa, and ordinary people who have loved in such a way that it has been like a rainstorm falling on the parched and dry earth.

This great stream is a river of life. This river of life flows and carries those who have loved us and taught us into the Christian faith. It is a continuing testament that God's grace is greater than our sin. This river of life carries all of our memories, of family and faith and grace and yes, even sin. This river of life flows through us, and it goes beyond us, and beyond even our vision of where it might lead. We do not even see its full effect, but in *hope* we believe that it flows to its source, to the throne of God and to the Lamb of Revelation 22.

When we touch the waters this morning, maybe, just maybe, if we have eyes to see and ears to hear, we see the dove flying over us and we hear the voice within us, "You are my son, you are my daughter, I am pleased with you." In the name of the Father who speaks to us, the Son who stands beside us, and the Holy Spirit who rests upon us. Amen.

For Spiritual Reflection and Further Learning
- Watch the films *Tender Mercies* and *Romero*.
- Think of a baptismal experience that was humorous or stressful, or one that did not go according to plan.
- Why is renunciation an important element in baptism?

RIVER OF LIFE

John 3:3-5; Matthew 28:16-20

When we celebrate the confirmation of young people, one of the questions we ask them, if they have been baptized, is if they remember their baptism—most do not—and if they know *where* they were baptized. Some can answer that question. We ask them to talk with their parents about the day of their baptism.

Some of us were baptized as adults, and some of us were baptized as children. Someone made the wonderful remark that "all baptisms are infant baptisms"—it is all grace, a gift we receive from our heavenly Lord. It connects us with Jesus, standing in the Jordan River, the river of life, being baptized by John, the heavens opening, the Voice saying, to him, "You are my son, I am pleased with you."

It doesn't matter whether you have been to the Jordan River, or whether you had water poured over you, or whether you walked down into a baptismal tank—I've done all of those things with people. What matters is whether you have been baptized. Early in my ministry I went to a revival meeting. Our choir was singing and I had been invited, and the evangelist was talking about something—he had gone a little astray from the subject, I think, but it was a hot summer evening and we were in no hurry to go back outside—and the evangelist decided to say something about baptism, and he said, "If you don't know Jesus, all the water in the world won't save you." I think he was talking about the *un*importance of baptism.

Of course, he was very wrong. It is not that God needs the baptism. That is pretty much what John says to Jesus, in the water. "I need to be baptized by you, and you come to me?" Jesus doesn't need to be washed, but we do. Jesus doesn't need to be cleansed, but we do, and so he stands in the river of life *with* us and *for* us. The early Christians remembered that. The baptism of Jesus is in all four Gospels. The story of the Good Samaritan is in only one of the Gospels. The Prodigal Son is in only one of the Gospels. Jesus washing the disciples' feet is in only one of the Gospels. The baptism of Jesus is in all four Gospels. Why? We all tend to forget! The early Christians needed to recall the significance of baptism. "Remember your baptism," we say in the liturgy, "and be thankful."

Of course, remembering our baptism is also remembering Christ: his life, his death, his resurrection. He stands in the river of life, the One who knew no sin takes our sin upon himself, and so he also stands in the river of pain, and the river of love.

I grew up in Georgia, and one of our contributions to the world has been the collected short stories of Flannery O'Connor. She was a woman of fierce artistic vision and deep Christian faith. She died of lupus at a relatively young age. In her short story "The River," she paints a picture of a preacher standing about ten feet out into a stream, with water up to his knees. He called out to the people:

> *"Maybe I know why you come," he said in the twangy voice, "maybe I don't.*
>
> *"If you ain't come for Jesus, you ain't come for me. If you just come to see can you leave your pain in the river, you ain't come for Jesus. You can't leave your pain in the river, he said. "I never told nobody that."*
>
> *("The River," A Good Man Is Hard to Find, by Flannery O'Connor [New York: Harcourt, Brace & World, Inc., © 1955 by Flannery O'Connor], 40)*

He speaks of a river of life, composed of Jesus' blood, a river in which a person can empty the pain of life, a river that flows toward the kingdom of Christ.

When we come to the waters of baptism, we stand in the river of pain, in the river of life. The river of pain reminds us of the necessity of new birth, of which Jesus spoke to Nicodemus. The river of pain is the coming alongside those who are in crisis, in grief, in trouble, in confusion. Pastors, lay caregivers, Stephen Ministers know what it is like to stand in this river of pain. And of course, this river of pain becomes a river of life: the breaking of water leads to new life; the giving of spiritual friendship and support creates an environment of new possibilities.

The river of life cannot be contained in our own lives, but flows into the lives of others, and so Jesus sends us forth to make disciples, to teach and to baptize. Parents have their child baptized, a son or daughter. They teach the faith to them. The congregation supports this. A young man or woman sits in the congregation and listens and wrestles with a call to full-time Christian service, and shares gifts as a Sunday school teacher or a servant among the homeless, and now goes forth to baptize and to teach and to make disciples.

One of the wonderful meanings of the baptism of a child is that the river does not begin with us—we are not the source, but we step into the river and the river carries us along. When we recite the baptismal liturgy, we are reminded that . . .

- The spirit of God moved over the face of the waters and brought forth life.
- God led Israel from slavery to freedom by passing through the waters.
- God took the water of Mary's womb and the Holy Spirit, and gave us the Savior.
- God spoke to Jesus as he stood in the Jordan and claimed him as his own.

God is still at work in the world, God still uses this gift of water to make us clean, to give us life, to claim *us* as his own. "If you ain't come for Jesus," the preacher said, "you ain't come for me." We come this morning to seek Jesus. We stand in the river of pain, the river of love, the river of life. And the best news is that Jesus stands in this water, *with* us and *for* us. And we, too, listen for the Voice, for a Word spoken to him and to all who will follow: "You are my child. I am pleased with you."

And so we pray: "O God, pour out your Holy Spirit to bless this gift of water and those who receive it, to wash away our sins and clothe us in righteousness throughout our lives that dying and being raised with Christ, we may share in his final victory."

Remember your baptism, and be thankful!

For Spiritual Reflection and Further Learning

- Read the Flannery O'Connor short story "The River," in the collection *A Good Man Is Hard to Find and Other Stories*.
- In your congregation, and in your own experience, where is the "river of pain"?
- In your congregation, and in your own experience, where is the "river of life"?

MAKE DISCIPLES

Matthew 28:16-20

It begins with the matter of *authority*. God gives authority to Jesus; Jesus gives this authority to his disciples. The source of any power or authority that we have can be traced back to the origin, to God, through Jesus Christ.

"The authority is given to me," Jesus says, "therefore go." The disciples, like Abraham before them, hear the voice sending them, the authorizing voice, just as we have listened to some voice—maybe the voices of our parents, maybe the voices of our teachers, maybe the voice of God.

The voice always calls us from where we have been to where we are going. From the beginning we have been sent—sent out. *Go*, and *make disciples*. That is our mission as followers of Jesus: to make disciples.

Baptism and confirmation, the Christian life is always a process, a journey. To keep going we need disciplines. The call gets us started. Baptism is one mark of that call. The disciplines keep us going. There is a connection between what we hear from God and how we respond to what we have heard. Is there a resonance between the call from God, the call to others, and our way of life? Is it real?

Sometimes the answer is *no*. "Not everyone who says to me, 'Lord, Lord,' will enter the kingdom" (Matthew 7:21a).

But at other times, with the help of God, the answer is *yes*. "Everyone then who hears these words of mine and acts on them," Jesus says, "will be like a wise man who built his house on rock" (Matthew 7:24).

The call and the disciplined life we see most clearly in Jesus. John baptized him, according to Matthew 3, and there he heard the call of God. He tested this call in the wilderness (chapter 4). Matthew tells us, in the Sermon on the Mount (chapters 5-7), that the people were amazed because Jesus "taught them as one having authority, and not as their scribes" (7:29). Jesus had the *form* of godliness, and he also had the *power*. And so as Christians we learn the rituals of our faith, but we also experience their inner meaning. That is where the power resides.

This power fueled Jesus' mission: *to make disciples.* We too are called to make disciples, sent to make disciples. Pastors are called or sent to places where we are not known, in the hope that people will sense a call and see a disciplined life in us, and recognize an authority beyond the laying on of a bishop's hands. We will need that authority, if we are going to make disciples. People will need to see, with clarity, the call and disciplined life of Jesus if they are to become his disciples. And so it is not about us, our call, our disciplines, but his call, his disciplined life—"he must increase," John testifies, "I must decrease" (John 3:30).

"Go and make disciples," Jesus says, "of all nations." The *ethne*— the Gentiles, the ethnics. Of course the dominant group defines who the *ethnics* are; of course we are all ethnics. Go not just to the lost sheep of the house of Israel (Matthew 15:24); that had been his mission, but now it expands. Maybe we go into all the world; maybe the world comes to us. A pastor walks through the church building on a Sunday evening and realizes that there is a Korean congregation meeting, a Brazilian fellowship meeting, the youth are singing down the hall, the chapel service is about to begin, and a chamber group is in the sanctuary—each a different world. Maybe we go out into the world; maybe the world comes to us!

We do sometimes make an error here. It is not that the world shapes our agenda. The agenda is clear in the five books of the Law (Genesis through Deuteronomy), and in the Gospel of Matthew: *the church shapes the agenda of the world.* At its best, the church does not withhold its agenda from any sector of the world.

I remember a young man who was a part of our church. He was a teenage boy, whose clothing consisted of one color: black. His face was covered with lipstick and rouge; his hero was Marilyn Manson. We hosted the youth at our parsonage after they had gone Christmas caroling, about thirty or forty of them squeezed into every room, and he was there, dressed in black, some kind of collar around his neck. I didn't even want to imagine the symbolism of it all. When I said hello, he glared at me. He was often around, usually with his friend, who was in our youth group. The two were always together in youth functions, and I would see them sitting in worship.

Almost a year later, I ran into him coming out of the church and he had on a blue shirt—light blue—the collar was gone, and his face looked different. He explained to me that he had become a Christian. It was an amazing conversation.

A few weeks later I ran into the mother of his best friend. I had to say to her, "I am impressed that through all that time your family hung in there with this guy who seemed so different, and even a little dangerous. That is quite a witness." And the mom responded, "We just figured that we had more power to change him than he had to change us."

That is witness. We are here because someone has witnessed to us, and we are always listening for some kind of witness, to a power that can change us, forgive us, heal us, and make us into a new creation. *The United Methodist Book of Discipline* asks the question of those who feel called to full-time Christian service: Do they know God as a pardoning God? That mom knew a pardoning God, she trusted in the power of a pardoning God, and so do we. And that is the source of any power we preachers have in the pulpit, and that is the purpose of any call we have to preach and teach.

"Go therefore and make disciples of all nations . . ." (Matthew 28:19). Jesus sends us out into the world, not to conform to the world, but to shape the world into the image of Christ. This good news is not just for us; it is for all people, even those who seem different and a little dangerous.

"Go therefore and make disciples of all nations, baptizing them in the name of the Father and of the Son and of the Holy Spirit . . ." The Trinitarian doctrines had not been worked out at this stage in the early church, but the names have a meaning nonetheless. Surely the disciples would have known the story of Jesus' baptism, which, in Matthew, comes just prior to his calling them to follow in Matthew 4. The voice of the Father—an affirming, blessing voice; the descent of the Dove—an empowering, encouraging sign; and the obedience of the Son—who hears, who stands in the waters for us and for all who would come later.

And so we baptize in order to bless, to affirm, to empower, to point to future obedience. We baptize in order to keep the family lineage going, a family line that transcends race and gender and class (see Galatians 3).

"Baptize," Jesus says, "and [teach] them to obey everything that I have commanded you" (Matthew 28:20). There is a place for a summary of what we believe—in Matthew it is in the Sermon on the Mount—there is a need to translate the beliefs of the past into the practices of the present—"you have heard it said, but I say to you." And that is all we ask here: that you begin to understand the content of all that Jesus commands— to seek the kingdom of God, to love one another as God has loved us, to announce the forgiveness of sins in God's name, to make the cross visible—costly grace, but grace still, both demand and gift. The one who said, "unless your righteousness exceeds that of the scribes and Pharisees, you will never enter the kingdom of heaven" (Matthew 5:20), also said, "Come to me, all you that are weary and are carrying heavy burdens, and I will give you rest . . . my yoke is easy, and my burden is light" (Matthew 11:28-30).

We believe in the grace of Jesus Christ, a free gift, and yet a grace that calls for lifelong, disciplined response. It is a wonderful gift to be confirmed, to be a Christian, to be a member of this church. It is demanding—prayers, presence, gifts, service. It is demanding because lives are at stake. I sense urgency in the last words of Jesus to the disciples. And yet there is one last word, a promise: "I am with you always . . ." (Matthew 28:20).

Thomas G. Long, in his commentary on Matthew, gets it right:

> *There was only one word that could have prevented them from col-*
> *lapsing in laughter or racing away in fear at the enormity of the mis-*
> *sion, only one word that could have strengthened their resolve and*
> *sent them out to the vast and forbidding world carrying only the*
> *gospel, and that was the word that Jesus spoke, "And remember, I*
> *am with you always, even to the end of the age."*
> (Matthew (Westminster Bible Companion) [Louisville: West-
> minster John Knox Press, © 1997 Thomas G. Long], 327)

The early Christians had lost their "missionary nerve" (see Mortimer Arias and Alan Johnson, *The Great Commission: Biblical Models for Evangelism* [Nashville: Abingdon Press, 1992], 34). Matthew's community was not a utopia. The weeds and the wheat were growing up together, the bad threatening to choke out the good (Matthew 13:24). There were false prophets and people who misrepresented themselves; hypocrites, who were not what they seemed to be. The community needed the clarity and confidence of a mission in the world. They needed to remember what that meant for them and for the world. In the life of Jesus, and in his last words, they were reminded of a call, a disciplined life, a witness, a teaching. We need these reminders. When we support those who are being baptized, who are being confirmed, when we stand alongside them, we are saying, "We will remind you."

The disciples heard the call of Jesus in their lives and they must have asked how they could possibly do all that God was calling them to do. Then they remembered the promise: "I am with you always, to the end of the age."

It turns out that was all they needed. It turns out that is all we need.

For Spiritual Reflection and Further Learning
- Consult the sources used for this sermon: Thomas G. Long, *Matthew (Westminster Bible Companion)*; Mortimer Arias and Alan Johnson, *The Great Commission: Biblical Models for Evangelism.*
- Compare the endings of the four Gospels.
- How does your church make disciples?
- Think of a person whose life has been transformed by the grace of a pardoning God. Give thanks to God for that person.

PART THREE

PRAYERS OF THANKSGIVING OVER THE WATER

I t is appropriate that we offer thanksgiving to God for the waters of baptism. In doing so, we are acknowledging God's presence, aware that God makes life (and new life) possible. These prayers of thanksgiving are offered as models for services related to particular biblical themes, seasons of the church year, and other occasions.

Each prayer of thanksgiving has a Trinitarian pattern—Father, Son, and Holy Spirit—(see Matthew 28), although the language can be adapted in particular settings. By following this pattern, the worshiping community, over time, becomes familiar with the history of God's mission in the world.

The prayers of thanksgiving should be prefaced by questions of the person being baptized (youth or adult), or of the parents (when a child is being baptized). The prayers are followed by the act of baptism itself, and then by some kind of congregational response.

These prayers can also be adapted for services of reaffirmation of baptismal vows, or for small group settings where baptism is a focus.

The responses of the worshiping community point to the reality that baptism is a corporate act; it is never merely a private experience. We are baptized into the body of Christ, into the salvation history of God who is creator, redeemer, sustainer and Father, Son, and Holy Spirit.

BIBLICAL THEMES

Creation

The Lord be with you.
And also with you.
Let us pray.
Eternal God,
In the beginning you created the heavens and the earth,
Your spirit moved over the face of the waters.
You separated earth from sky, water from dry land,
Light from darkness.
You filled the earth with your creatures,
And created us, male and female in your image.
You saw everything that you had made, and called it good.
In the fullness of time,
You entered into our world in Jesus Christ,
Who had from the beginning lived with you,
And through whom all things were made.
In him was life, and the life was the light of all people.
The light shines in the darkness,
And the darkness has not overcome it.
The word became flesh, full of grace and truth.
Pour out your Holy Spirit,
Which moved over the face of the waters in creation,
Which bears witness to the living presence of Jesus Christ,
To bless this gift of water, and those who receive it,
That our sins may be washed away,
That we may be reminded that we are your good creation,
That we live as grateful stewards and faithful disciples.
Glory to the Father, and to the Son, and to the Holy Spirit.

The Flood

The Lord be with you.
And also with you.
Let us pray.
Eternal God,
When the earth was filled with pain, suffering, and evil,
And the human condition grieved your heart,
You cleansed the earth with a great flood.
You made a covenant with Noah,
Sent a dove after the waters had subsided,
And set in the clouds a rainbow.
The earth is the Lord's.
Because we rejected your laws and resisted the words of your
       prophets,
And the human condition grieved your heart,
You sent Jesus to live, to die, and to rise again,
And in him you made a new covenant with us.
His righteousness covers all of our sin.
In the name of Jesus Christ, we are forgiven.
Pour out your Holy Spirit,
To bless this gift of water, and those who receive it,
To renew the creation and to guide us in the way of the Lord.
As we have died with Christ, may we also rise with him.
As we have been plunged into the waters of the cleansing
       flood,
May we live in the brilliance of the rainbow,
A sign of your everlasting love for us.
Glory be to the Father, and to the Son,
       and to the Holy Spirit.

Crossing the Sea

The Lord be with you.
And also with you.
Let us pray.
Eternal God,
When your people journeyed from slavery to freedom,

They came to the seashore, pursued by their enemies.
You parted the waters
By the mighty power of your Spirit
And your children passed safely to the other side.
Surely it is God who saves us.
In the fullness of time
Your Son Jesus Christ came to show us
The way that leads to life,
To rescue us from slavery to sin and death.
As we trust in him,
You lead us and guide us into a relationship with you.
He is the way, the truth, and the life.
Pour out your Holy Spirit,
To bless this gift of water and those who receive it.
Let this water be a reminder of your mighty works
Among our ancestors,
Who were bound for the Promised Land,
Who have gathered at the river,
And whose trust in you has led them to freedom.
Glory to the Father, and to the Son, and to the Holy Spirit.

The Birth of Jesus

The Lord be with you.
And also with you.
Let us pray.
Eternal God,
Throughout all generations you have moved
        among your people,
In the lives of Abraham and Sarah, David and Ruth,
        prophets and priests.
Your word and your way of life
Has been passed from generation to generation.
In triumph and adversity,
In faithfulness and apostasy,
In praise and lamentation,
You have kept your covenant with us.

The steadfast love of the Lord is from everlasting to everlasting.
In the fullness of time you gave your only Son to be our savior.
His name would be called Jesus,
For he would save his people from their sins.
He was born to Joseph and Mary,
in the midst of shepherds,
and he was visited by the Magi.
He would grow up to be the Good Shepherd,
And his life would be a light to the nations.
Glory to God in the highest, and on earth peace.
Pour out your Holy Spirit,
To bless this gift of water and those who receive it.
Let this water be a sign of our rebirth,
In remembrance of the birth of the Messiah,
The Prince of Peace.
And may your blessing continue from generation to
generation.
The steadfast love of the Lord is from everlasting to everlasting.

The Baptism of Jesus

The Lord be with you.
And also with you.
Let us pray.
Eternal God,
In a time of chaos,
Your spirit moved over the face of the waters
And you caused light to shine in the darkness.
In a time of evil,
Your waters cleansed the earth in a great flood.
In a time of danger, you allowed your people to
pass through the waters of the sea.
Praise to you, O God of power and might.
In the fullness of time you sent your servant John
To baptize Jesus in the Jordan River.

He saw your spirit descending upon him,
In the form of a dove,
The light of the sky shining upon him.
You spoke words of blessing to him:
"This is my beloved Son, in him I am well pleased."
Spirit of God, descend upon our hearts.
Pour out your Holy Spirit,
To bless this gift of water and those who receive it.
May we feel your presence in this holy time.
May we see your light shining upon us.
And may we hear your words of blessing:
This is my beloved child,
In him or her I am well pleased.
Glory be to the Father, and to the Son,
      and to the Holy Spirit.

The Great Commission

The Lord be with you.
And also with you.
Let us pray.
Eternal God,
Creator of all that is, seen and unseen,
You created a people to declare your glory among all people
And made a covenant with Abraham:
You blessed him to be a blessing,
And promised that in him all the families of the earth would
      be blessed.
You commanded your people
To be a light to the nations.
Make a joyful noise to the Lord, all the earth!
In Jesus Christ,
You came first to your chosen people,
Teaching, healing, announcing the Kingdom.
Yet his life would be given for all people,
And his commission to his closest followers
Was to make disciples of all nations,

Baptizing them in the name of the Father, the Son, and the
	Holy Spirit.
**Every knee shall bow, every tongue shall confess that
	Jesus Christ is Lord.**
Pour out your Holy Spirit,
To bless this gift of water and those who receive it.
As you gave the promise to your disciples,
"I am with you always, even to the end of the age,"
May the one who is baptized know the assurance of your
		presence,
to be with him or her through all the days of his or her life.
May this your child grow into the fullness of faith and
	obedience
	to your great commission,
As a disciple of Jesus Christ.
**Glory be to the Father, and the Son, and the Holy Spirit.
	Amen.**

I Will Pour Out My Spirit

The Lord be with you.
And also with you.
Let us pray.
Eternal Father,
You give life to the world
In the beauty of creation, in the liberation from slavery,
In the boundaries of the law, in the wisdom of the prophets.
Your power and wisdom deliver us from evil.
Your grace and mercy save us from death.
You promise to be near to us,
Filling us with your steadfast love.
We give thanks for the good news of your prophecy:
"I will pour out my spirit on all flesh."
Come, Holy Spirit.
In Jesus Christ,
You come in the flesh, the new creation,

The mighty Savior, the fulfillment of the law and the
      prophets.
Though he was rich,
Yet for our sakes he became poor.
Though he was in the form of God,
Yet for our sakes he took on our human nature.
His life was poured out, an offering, a sacrifice,
For us.
Come, Lord Jesus.
Pour out your Holy Spirit,
To bless this gift of water and those who receive it.
Pour out your Holy Spirit on all flesh,
And especially on this your child.
May he or she know your power, your mercy,
Your grace, your wisdom.
May these words be even now
A sign of your new creation.
Grant your blessing upon this your child, we pray.
**Send forth your spirit, and we shall be created,
and you shall renew the face of the earth.**

Baptized into His Death
The Lord be with you.
And also with you.
Let us pray.
Eternal Father,
Across the centuries your people have tasted the sweetness of
      victory
  and the bitterness of suffering;
They have known the security of home and the chaos of
      exile;
They have pleased you with faithfulness,
  and disappointed you with their disobedience.
They have remembered your mighty works and worshiped
      only you;
They have neglected the faith, and worshiped other gods.

I have set before you life and death, blessing and curse.
In Jesus Christ, you show us victory through suffering.
In Jesus Christ, you show us faithfulness and obedience.
In Jesus Christ, you are glorified by mighty works of
    compassion.
In Jesus Christ, we are rescued from the far country, and
    gathered
  into the embrace of the Waiting Lord.
Buried with him in baptism, we will be raised in glory.
Pour out your Holy Spirit,
To bless this gift of water and those who receive it.
As we have died with Christ in baptism,
May we also live with him in service and witness.
As we have walked with him in suffering,
May we also live with him in glory.
May the Spirit guide us into the truth that shall set us free,
And may we walk in newness of life.
Glory to the Father, and to the Son,
    and to the Holy Spirit.

One Faith, One Lord, One Baptism

The Lord be with you.
And also with you.
Let us pray.
Eternal Father,
You created all people in your image
And breathed into them the breath of life.
You gathered numerous tribes into one family,
To worship and serve one God.
You made a covenant with Israel,
And called them to faithful obedience and steadfast witness.
Hear O Israel, the Lord our God is one.
In Jesus Christ, there is a new creation.
He called his disciples to observe your commandments,
To worship you in spirit and in truth,
To remember the covenant you had made with our ancestors.

He is the way, the truth, and the life.
**You shall love the Lord your God with all your heart
And mind and soul and strength.**
Pour out your Holy Spirit
Which created one family on the day of Pentecost,
And bless this gift of water.
This day, your child is baptized into one body—
Jew or Greek, male or female, slave or free.
There is one faith, one Lord, one baptism,
One God and Father of us all.
In the unity of the spirit make us one in Christ Jesus.
**Glory to the Father, and to the Son,
          and to the Holy Spirit.**

The River of Life

The Lord be with you.
And also with you.
Let us pray.
Eternal God,
In the beginning you separated the waters from dry land,
Bringing forth fruit from the earth,
Creating every kind of animal that swims in the seas
And flies through the air and races across the earth,
And you called your creation good.
You created us, male and female, in your image.
The earth is the Lord's, and all that is in it.
In Jesus Christ you came to renew your image in us.
He was baptized in the Jordan River,
Standing in the waters to fulfill all righteousness,
The heavens opening, the dove descending,
Your voice speaking,
"This is my Son, the beloved, I am pleased with him."
As we baptize this child of yours, O God,
We see the vision of a river of the water of life,
That flows from the Throne of God and of the Lamb.
We see the tree of life standing on either side of the river,

As the heavens open, we worship you,
Asking that you would pour out your Spirit on this gift of
      water,
And this child of yours, who receives it.
He or she has been created in your image,
Washed clean by these waters,
Sealed with your Spirit.
**Glory be to the Father, and to the Son,
    and to the Holy Spirit.**

THE CHURCH YEAR

Advent

The Lord be with you.
And also with you.
Let us pray.
Eternal God,
When nothing existed but chaos
You swept across the dark waters
And brought forth light.
After the flood you sent in the clouds a rainbow.
When you saw your people as slaves in Egypt,
You led them to freedom through the sea.
Their children you brought through the Jordan
To the land which you promised.
Sing to the Lord all the earth, tell of God's mercy each day.
As the time drew near, your prophets came announcing the
      good news
That you would bring comfort to your people,
An end to captivity and warfare,
That the year of the Lord's favor was at hand.
Your messenger prepared the way,
Baptizing with water,
But pointing to One greater than he,
Who would baptize with the Holy Spirit.

**Declare his works to the nations, his glory among all the
people.**
Pour out your Holy Spirit,
To bless this gift of water and those who receive it,
To wash away their sin
And clothe them in righteousness throughout their lives,
That dying and being raised with Christ,
They may share in his final victory.
**All praise to you, Eternal Father,
Through your Son Jesus Christ,
Who with you and the Holy Spirit
Lives and reigns forever. Amen.**

Christmas

The Lord be with you.
And also with you.
Let us pray.
Eternal God,
When nothing existed but chaos
You swept across the dark waters
And brought forth light.
After the flood you sent in the clouds a rainbow.
When you saw your people as slaves in Egypt,
You led them to freedom through the sea.
Their children you brought through the Jordan
To the land which you promised.
Sing to the Lord all the earth, tell of God's mercy each day.
In the fullness of time you entered into this world
In Jesus, born of Mary and Joseph,
The word made flesh, full of grace and truth.
His birth in Bethlehem was good news of great joy for all
people.
He was the light coming into the world,
The long anticipated Messiah,
The Savior, Christ the Lord.
Glory to God in the highest, and on earth, peace.

Pour out your Holy Spirit,
To bless this gift of water and those who receive it,
To wash away their sin
And clothe them in righteousness throughout their lives,
That dying and being raised with Christ,
They may share in his final victory.
All praise to you, Eternal Father,
Through your Son Jesus Christ,
Who with you and the Holy Spirit
Lives and reigns forever. Amen.

Epiphany

The Lord be with you.
And also with you.
Let us pray.
Eternal God,
When nothing existed but chaos
You swept across the dark waters
And brought forth light.
After the flood you sent in the clouds a rainbow.
When you saw your people as slaves in Egypt,
You led them to freedom through the sea.
Their children you brought through the Jordan
To the land which you promised.
Sing to the Lord all the earth, tell of God's mercy each day.
After Jesus was born in Bethlehem,
Herod received word of the greatness of this child, and was
   threatened.
He commissioned the wise men
To go to the Christ-child, and when they were in the pres-
   ence of Jesus,
They were overwhelmed with joy.
They offered him gifts, gold, frankincense, and myrrh;
And then they returned not to Herod,
But to their own country.

Declare his works to the nations, his glory among all the
    people.
Pour out your Holy Spirit,
To bless this gift of water and those who receive it,
To wash away their sin
And clothe them in righteousness throughout their lives,
That dying and being raised with Christ,
They may share in his final victory.
All praise to you, Eternal Father,
Through your Son Jesus Christ,
Who with you and the Holy Spirit
Lives and reigns forever. Amen.

Baptism of the Lord

The Lord be with you.
And also with you.
Let us pray.
Eternal God,
When nothing existed but chaos
You swept across the dark waters
And brought forth light.
After the flood you sent in the clouds a rainbow.
When you saw your people as slaves in Egypt,
You led them to freedom through the sea.
Their children you brought through the Jordan
To the land which you promised.
Sing to the Lord all the earth, tell of God's mercy each day.
Your servant John came preaching repentance
For the forgiveness of sins.
Jesus met John, at the Jordan River,
And was baptized by him, to fulfill all righteousness.
In his baptism, the heavens opened,
A dove descended upon him, and a voice from heaven spoke,
"This is my Son, the beloved, with whom I am well pleased."
God is light, and in him is no darkness.
Pour out your Holy Spirit,

To bless this gift of water and those who receive it,
To wash away their sin
And clothe them in righteousness throughout their lives,
That dying and being raised with Christ,
They may share in his final victory.
All praise to you, Eternal Father,
Through your Son Jesus Christ,
Who with you and the Holy Spirit
Lives and reigns forever. Amen.

Transfiguration

The Lord be with you.
And also with you.
Let us pray.
Eternal God,
When nothing existed but chaos
You swept across the dark waters
And brought forth light.
After the flood you sent in the clouds a rainbow.
When you saw your people as slaves in Egypt,
You led them to freedom through the sea.
Their children you brought through the Jordan
To the land which you promised.
Sing to the Lord all the earth, tell of God's mercy each day.
Jesus went with the disciples, Peter, James, and John,
To a mountaintop. There Jesus was transfigured,
And he appeared in dazzling white.
He stood with Moses and Elijah, representing the law and
    the prophets.
A voice spoke from the cloud,
"This is my Son, the Beloved; listen to him."
And then only Jesus was present.
We see the light of the gospel in the glory of Christ,
Who is the image of God.
Pour out your Holy Spirit,
To bless this gift of water and those who receive it,

To wash away their sin
And clothe them in righteousness throughout their lives,
That dying and being raised with Christ,
They may share in his final victory.
All praise to you, Eternal Father,
Through your Son Jesus Christ,
Who with you and the Holy Spirit
Lives and reigns forever. Amen.

Lent

The Lord be with you.
And also with you.
Let us pray.
Eternal God,
When nothing existed but chaos
You swept across the dark waters
And brought forth light.
After the flood you sent in the clouds a rainbow.
When you saw your people as slaves in Egypt,
You led them to freedom through the sea.
Their children you brought through the Jordan
To the land which you promised.
Sing to the Lord all the earth, tell of God's mercy each day.
We were once dead through our trespasses and sins,
And yet we have been made alive in Jesus Christ.
God proves his love toward us in that while we were yet
        sinners,
Christ died for us. Indeed, God so loved the world
That he gave his only Son, that whoever believes in him
Would not perish, but have eternal life.
Declare his works to the nations, his glory among all the
        people.
Pour out your Holy Spirit,
To bless this gift of water and those who receive it,
To wash away their sin
And clothe them in righteousness throughout their lives,

That dying and being raised with Christ,
They may share in his final victory.
All praise to you, Eternal Father,
Through your Son Jesus Christ,
Who with you and the Holy Spirit
Lives and reigns forever. Amen.

Passion Sunday

The Lord be with you.
And also with you.
Let us pray.
Eternal God,
When nothing existed but chaos
You swept across the dark waters
And brought forth light.
After the flood you sent in the clouds a rainbow.
When you saw your people as slaves in Egypt,
You led them to freedom through the sea.
Their children you brought through the Jordan
To the land which you promised.
Sing to the Lord all the earth, tell of God's mercy each day.
We remember Jesus, who though he was in the form of God,
Did not regard equality with God as something to be
        exploited,
But he emptied himself, taking the form of a servant,
And in humility was obedient to the point of death,
Even death on a cross. Therefore God has highly exalted him
And given him the name that is above every name,
So that every knee shall bow and every tongue confess.
Jesus Christ is Lord, to the glory of God the Father.
Pour out your Holy Spirit,
To bless this gift of water and those who receive it,
To wash away their sin
And clothe them in righteousness throughout their lives,
That dying and being raised with Christ,
They may share in his final victory.

All praise to you, Eternal Father,
Through your Son Jesus Christ,
Who with you and the Holy Spirit
Lives and reigns forever. Amen.

Easter

The Lord be with you.
And also with you.
Let us pray.
Eternal God,
When nothing existed but chaos
You swept across the dark waters
And brought forth light.
After the flood you sent in the clouds a rainbow.
When you saw your people as slaves in Egypt,
You led them to freedom through the sea.
Their children you brought through the Jordan
To the land which you promised.
Sing to the Lord all the earth, tell of God's mercy each day.
Christ died for our sins, in accordance with the Scriptures.
He was buried.
On the third day he was raised from the dead,
In accordance with the Scriptures.
He appeared to the women,
To the disciples, to more than five hundred followers.
He is alive, and he stands among us.
Death no longer has dominion over us.
The Lord has risen. The Lord has risen indeed!
Alleluia! Christ has risen!
Pour out your Holy Spirit,
To bless this gift of water and those who receive it,
To wash away their sin
And clothe them in righteousness throughout their lives,
That dying and being raised with Christ,
They may share in his final victory.
All praise to you, Eternal Father,

Through your Son Jesus Christ,
Who with you and the Holy Spirit
Lives and reigns forever. Amen.

Pentecost

The Lord be with you.
And also with you.
Let us pray.
Eternal God,
When nothing existed but chaos
You swept across the dark waters
And brought forth light.
After the flood you sent in the clouds a rainbow.
When you saw your people as slaves in Egypt,
You led them to freedom through the sea.
Their children you brought through the Jordan
To the land which you promised.
Sing to the Lord all the earth, tell of God's mercy each day.
Jesus promised that, when he left us, we would be given a
        comforter.
Jesus promised, as he ascended, that we would receive the
        power through the Holy Spirit.
On the day of Pentecost, you poured this gift
Upon your people,
Even as Jesus poured out his life for us.
On the day of Pentecost, you poured out your spirit
On all flesh, just as Jesus had commanded his followers
To go into the world and make disciples.
Declare his works to the nations, his glory among all the
        people.
Pour out your Holy Spirit, on this Pentecost
To bless this gift of water and those who receive it,
To wash away their sin,
To make all of your believers one,
And clothe them in righteousness throughout their lives,
That dying and being raised with Christ,

They may share in his final victory.
All praise to you, Eternal Father,
Through your Son Jesus Christ,
Who with you and the Holy Spirit
Lives and reigns forever. Amen.

Trinity Sunday

The Lord be with you.
And also with you.
Let us pray.
Eternal God,
When nothing existed but chaos
You swept across the dark waters
And brought forth light.
After the flood you sent in the clouds a rainbow.
When you saw your people as slaves in Egypt,
You led them to freedom through the sea.
Their children you brought through the Jordan
To the land which you promised.
Sing to the Lord all the earth, tell of God's mercy each day.
We gather in the grace of our Lord Jesus Christ.
He was led by the Spirit to proclaim your word.
He prayed to the Father for strength, for assurance,
        for guidance.
As he was sent by the Father, so he sent his disciples into the
        world,
In the power of the Spirit. He commanded his followers
To make disciples, baptizing them in the name of the Father,
The Son, and the Holy Spirit.
He gave us guidance and assurance, saying,
"I am with you always, to the end of the age."
Pour out your Holy Spirit,
To bless this gift of water and those who receive it,
To wash away their sin
And clothe them in righteousness throughout their lives,
That dying and being raised with Christ,

They may share in his final victory.
All praise to you, Eternal Father,
Through your Son Jesus Christ,
Who with you and the Holy Spirit
Lives and reigns forever. Amen.

All Saints

The Lord be with you.
And also with you.
Let us pray.
Eternal God,
When nothing existed but chaos
You swept across the dark waters
And brought forth light.
After the flood you sent in the clouds a rainbow.
When you saw your people as slaves in Egypt,
You led them to freedom through the sea.
Their children you brought through the Jordan
To the land which you promised.
Sing to the Lord all the earth, tell of God's mercy each day.
When we are baptized in Christ's name,
We are given a glorious inheritance among the saints.
By our promises, or those who speak on our behalf,
We are marked by the seal of the Holy Spirit,
In anticipation of our redemption as God's own people,
To the praise of his glory.
With all of the saints who have gone before us,
We await the day in which we will stand in the presence
Of the Holy One.
Salvation belongs to our God, and to the Lamb who is
        seated on the throne.
Pour out your Holy Spirit, that we may see ourselves as
        saints.
Bless this gift of water and those who receive it,
To wash away their sin
And clothe them in righteousness throughout their lives,

That dying and being raised with Christ,
They may share in his final victory.
All praise to you, Eternal Father,
Through your Son Jesus Christ,
Who with you and the Holy Spirit
Lives and reigns forever. Amen.

Christ the King

The Lord be with you.
And also with you.
Let us pray.
Eternal God,
When nothing existed but chaos
You swept across the dark waters
And brought forth light.
After the flood you sent in the clouds a rainbow.
When you saw your people as slaves in Egypt,
You led them to freedom through the sea.
Their children you brought through the Jordan
To the land which you promised.
Sing to the Lord all the earth, tell of God's mercy each day.
In baptism we are given a visible sign of God's reign on this
       earth.
We are rescued from the powers of darkness
And transferred into the kingdom of his beloved Son.
In Jesus Christ all things in heaven and earth were created,
Visible or invisible.
He is before all things, and in him all things
Hold together. He is the head of the body, the church.
Through him God is reconciling all things, making peace
Through the blood of the cross.
Crown him with many crowns!
Pour out your Holy Spirit,
To bless this gift of water and those who receive it,
To wash away their sin
And clothe them in righteousness throughout their lives,

That dying and being raised with Christ the King,
They may share in his final victory.
All praise to you, Eternal Father,
Through your Son Jesus Christ,
Who with you and the Holy Spirit
Lives and reigns forever. Amen.

SPECIAL DAYS

New Year's Day

The Lord be with you.
And also with you.
Let us pray.
Eternal God,
When nothing existed but chaos
You swept across the dark waters
And brought forth light.
After the flood you sent in the clouds a rainbow.
When you saw your people as slaves in Egypt,
You led them to freedom through the sea.
Their children you brought through the Jordan
To the land which you promised.
Sing to the Lord all the earth, tell of God's mercy each day.
We remember that your Son Jesus Christ came announcing
        the Kingdom of God,
Calling us to repentance and belief.
As his followers we put aside all that is past,
And await the transformation of all that is to come.
We are his new creation, created for good works.
Through his death the sins of our past are washed away.
By his life the possibilities for our future are clearly before us.
"Behold," says the Lord, "I make all things new."
Pour out your Holy Spirit,
To bless this gift of water and those who receive it,
To wash away their sin

And clothe them in righteousness throughout their lives,
That dying and being raised with Christ the King,
They may share in his final victory.
All praise to you, Eternal Father,
Through your Son Jesus Christ,
Who with you and the Holy Spirit
Lives and reigns forever. Amen.

Martin Luther King Jr. Remembrance

The Lord be with you.
And also with you.
Let us pray.
Eternal God,
When nothing existed but chaos
You swept across the dark waters
And brought forth light.
After the flood you sent in the clouds a rainbow.
When you saw your people as slaves in Egypt,
You led them to freedom through the sea.
Their children you brought through the Jordan
To the land which you promised.
Sing to the Lord all the earth, tell of God's mercy each day.
In baptism we follow our Lord, who spoke against the
                powerful of his own day.
As his disciples, we are rescued from the powers of darkness
And transferred into the kingdom of his beloved Son.
We remember his servant Martin and all those who spoke
Against the powerful of their own times,
Boldly asking that you will deliver us from evil,
And confidently looking toward the time when
Justice will roll down like waters,
And righteousness like an everflowing stream.
Lead us, O God, into your Promised Land.
Pour out your Holy Spirit,
To bless this gift of water and those who receive it,
To wash away their sin

And clothe them in righteousness throughout their lives,
That dying and being raised with Christ the King,
They may share in his final victory.
All praise to you, Eternal Father,
Through your Son Jesus Christ,
Who with you and the Holy Spirit
Lives and reigns forever. Amen.

Earth Day

The Lord be with you.
And also with you.
Let us pray.
Eternal God,
When nothing existed but chaos
You swept across the dark waters,
And brought forth light.
You created all that is, and called it good.
After the flood you sent in the clouds a rainbow.
When you saw your people as slaves in Egypt,
You led them to freedom through the sea.
Their children you brought through the Jordan
To the land which you promised.
Sing to the Lord all the earth, tell of God's mercy each day.
Our lives depend upon your gift of water.
We remember that Jesus was nurtured in the water of a
        womb.
His disciples fished the waters of the Galilee.
He gave bread to those who were hungry,
And he commanded his disciples to give a cup of water in his
        name.
Your gift of water makes the harvest of food for the hungry
        possible in our own time.
Our lives depend upon this gift of water,
which is also a reminder of the gift of salvation
in Jesus Christ, who is the new creation.
The earth is the Lord's and all that is in it.

Pour out your Holy Spirit,
To bless this gift of water and those who receive it,
To wash away their sin
And clothe them in righteousness throughout their lives,
That dying and being raised with Christ the King,
They may share in his final victory.
All praise to you, Eternal Father,
Through your Son Jesus Christ,
Who with you and the Holy Spirit
Lives and reigns forever. Amen.

World Communion

The Lord be with you.
And also with you.
Let us pray.
Eternal God,
When nothing existed but chaos
You swept across the dark waters
And brought forth light.
After the flood you sent in the clouds a rainbow.
When you saw your people as slaves in Egypt,
You led them to freedom through the sea.
Their children you brought through the Jordan
To the land which you promised.
Sing to the Lord all the earth, tell of God's mercy each day.
When Jesus Christ was born, the Magi came from the East,
        bearing gifts.
He fed the multitudes and taught the crowds.
His life, death, and resurrection were for all people.
He commissioned his followers to make disciples of all
        nations.
His people are to be a light to the nations.
When we are baptized in his name, we become citizens of a
        kingdom
That transcends every nationality, language, and race.

**Declare his works to the nations, his glory among all the
people.**
Pour out your Holy Spirit,
To bless this gift of water and those who receive it,
To wash away their sin
And clothe them in righteousness throughout their lives,
That dying and being raised with Christ,
They may share in his final victory.
All praise to you, Eternal Father,
Through your Son Jesus Christ,
Who with you and the Holy Spirit
Lives and reigns forever. Amen.

Thanksgiving

The Lord be with you.
And also with you.
Let us pray.
Eternal God,
When nothing existed but chaos
You swept across the dark waters
And brought forth light.
After the flood you sent in the clouds a rainbow.
When you saw your people as slaves in Egypt,
You led them to freedom through the sea.
Their children you brought through the Jordan
To the land which you promised.
Sing to the Lord all the earth, tell of God's mercy each day.
The waters are your creation, O God.
In the water of a womb Jesus was nourished.
At the waters of the Galilee he called his disciples.
He promised to give living waters to those who thirst.
With water he washed the feet of the disciples.
For the gift of life, we praise you.
For the call to give life to others, we thank you.
Dwell within us, and fill us with a sense of thanksgiving
In the name and spirit of Jesus Christ.

He will guide us to springs of living water.
Pour out your Holy Spirit,
To bless this gift of water and those who receive it,
To wash away their sin
And clothe them in righteousness throughout their lives,
That dying and being raised with Christ the King,
They may share in his final victory.
All praise to you, Eternal Father,
Through your Son Jesus Christ,
Who with you and the Holy Spirit
Lives and reigns forever. Amen.